What People Are Saying

Are you guarding an inner truth? Take this journey with Grace and learn how to release your authentic self! Her essays show how living a genuine life requires - and enhances - humor, grit, self-awareness, empathy, courage, and kindness. I devour and save each of her blog posts as they come along, and I'm grateful that she's compiled them into this book. It will live long and prosper on my shelf!

– **Charlotte Pierce,** President, The Independent Publishers of New England; President, Pierce Press

Author Grace Anne Stevens has been sharing her journey toward living authentically in blog posts since 2015. Compiling these remarkable writings into 'Musing on Living Authentically,' she offers readers more than a glimpse into her experiences with finding her true self and revealing it; she offers a wide-open view, complete with doubts, fears, hopes, dreams, and an often startling self-awareness.

This is not merely a book for those in, or contemplating, gender transition. This is a book for everyone: Who am I, really? What must I do to become my truest self? And what might I find on the other side of the experiences that make up this road less traveled?

For living fully as we are, with its great rewards and its many challenges, is not a path taken often enough by any of us. Grace shows the way, with candor, humor, and the organic insights that come from discovery of both the self and the world in which the self seeks to survive and thrive. Grace does that with poise, determination and humor, and in finding her way, she shows us how to as well.

– **Mark McNease,** Editor and Publisher, lgbtSr.org

Musings on Living Authentically

Grace Anne Stevens

 Graceful Change Press • Lexington

Contact:

Grace Stevens

(781) 789-6103

gas333@verizon.net

www.graceannestevens.com

314 Bedford Street

Suite 105

Lexington MA 02420

"No! Maybe? Yes! Not Just a Transgender Memoir," interview with Grace Stevens used with permssion:

(http://www.opednews.com/articles/No-Maybe-Yes---Not-Ju-by-Joan-Brunwasser-Authenticity_Boston_Identity_Interviews-150706-331.html)

"Books Sure to Empower Women in the New Year,"
by Joan Schweighardt, used with permission:
http://everydaypowerblog.com/2015/12/17/eightbooks-sure-to-empower-womenin-the-new-year-2/

This book is dedicated to all those who
Have chosen,
Are choosing,
Or
Will choose
To live their true life.

I am Me. In all the world, there is no one else exactly like me. Everything that comes out of me is authentically mine, because I alone chose it. I own everything about me: my body, my feelings, my mouth, my voice, all my actions, whether they be to others or myself. I own my fantasies, my dreams, my hopes, my fears. I own my triumphs and successes, all my failures and mistakes. Because I own all of me, I can become intimately acquainted with me. By so doing, I can love me and be friendly with all my parts.

I know there are aspects about myself that puzzle me, and other aspects that I do not know, but as long as I am friendly and loving to myself, I can courageously and hopefully look for solutions to the puzzles and ways to find out more about me. However I look and sound, whatever I say and do, and whatever I think and feel at a given moment in time is authentically me. If later some parts of how I looked, sounded, thought, and felt turn out to be unfitting, I can discard that which is unfitting, keep the rest, and invent something new for that which I discarded. I can see, hear, feel, think, say, and do. I have the tools to survive, to be close to others, to be productive, and to make sense and order out of the world of people and things outside of me. I own me, and therefore, I can engineer me. I am me, and I am Okay."

– Virginia Satir

Contents

Foreword

My friendship with Grace Stevens began in 2015 when I read her blog post "Where is God?" in The Huffington Post. Unapologetically direct and yet with a profound sweetness, Grace writes about her faith and about what she sees as the limits of religion. I was struck particularly by the contrasting of the emptiness of the celebration of her bar mitzvah milestone as a thirteen year old who knew she was not really becoming a man and the blessing years later of being able to embrace her truth and proclaim "Today I am a woman." As a fellow blogger on The Huffington Post and a Rabbi, I was moved by her powerful words and shared with her my appreciation. Since then we have exchanged writings and availed ourselves of opportunities to connect on social media. It is my great honor to have been asked to contribute this foreword to Grace's musings on her personal journey

I have found in Grace's writing what I believe so many have also discovered: a powerful expression of what is at stake in living your authentic self. Her story is not simply an exploration of "What is it like to be transgender?" but rather "What does it mean to accept yourself and your experience of yourself as real?"

From a distance, questions about transgender people may seem like matters of faith or worldview, and for some, they may always be seen through such a lens. However, from inside a person's own story, gender is another way to recognize who we are—no more or less real than religion, sex, race, sexuality, or a myriad of other markers that cannot be pinned down definitively from the outside.

Grace's essays animate my perspective on my own Jewishness, a broad identity that she and I share, even though it manifests itself very differently in our lives. Her story speaks to me particularly as a person of faith. I find it somewhat ironic that the same faiths that teach that the intangible trumps that which can be seen in the world, have been so often called upon to deny legitimacy to those who know the wholeness of themselves regardless of what others insist about the parts of their body.

While labels and categorizations seem to be the currency of identity, overly defining ourselves and others hides an opportunity to discover a vital teaching. In seeing the authenticity in the unfolding life of another, we understand that there are multiple authentic truths. My unfolding life and identity is rendered more potently authentic as I learn yours.

When it comes to "real" we are to a certain extent programmed to look for the definitive yes or no. However, our own experiences and encounters with others belie the simplicity of a world divided into what is real and what is not. Whether race, religion, sexuality, mental state, health, nationality, gender, relationship...no person's identity lives separately from interpretation by others and even ourselves. As social media brings more and more of the world into our view, embracing the stories of other people's lives opens us to learn from the reality of others rather than impose our judgments on others.

Writing such as Grace's reinforces that who we are is personal and irreplaceable; a product more of stories in progress than labels and categories. I hope that Grace's reflections on what she calls her "transgender life" will find themselves into the consciousness of a wide variety of readers.

– Rabbi Michael Bernstein
Congregation Gesher L' Torah
Alpharetta, GA

Preface

A long time ago, I remember learning about the phrase credited to Rene Descartes:

Cogito ergo sum
I think, therefore I am

I am not the first person to take the journey to transition their gender. Nor will I be the last.

Our paths are all so different and ultimately unique. Perhaps the most common trait that we share is how much we feel alone and scared on our journeys.

It has taken me some time to understand these feelings are actually a fully human trait and not one that is reserved for trans people.I have been writing about "My Transgender Life," but I know that what I share is for everyone, and each person has their own stories that may be similar to the ones I share.

I think of this book as a compilation of my love letters to the universe.

You may want to write some of your reflections too.

My True Self

It may sound a bit surprising to some, and perhaps even outlandish to others, that the actual act of changing my gender from male to female was not the hardest part of my transition.

I know a number of people who have taken years to transition. Some were on hormones for some time as their body and skin slowly changed in ways that were noticeable to others. I am pretty sure that parts of them loved the changes, while there were other parts in strong denial that anyone else noticed. Many were not even aware how other people saw them as they wrestled whether they could actually cross that line called "transition."

That was not the path that I chose. I was 64 years old, with a bald dome, and sagging wattle that long ago was a smooth neck. When I cross-dressed and went out in public, I had no sense that I would be able to live my life fully as a female. I knew that first, if and then finally when I chose to transition, I could only do it if I had what is called facial feminization surgery, or FFS. For me this was a nine-hour procedure that required four weeks of healing. My transition at work was a step function. I left work for four weeks, with only a select group of managers knowing what I was doing, as they were all told that this was strictly confidential. My coworkers were not told, and some tried to contact me to find out if I was OK. I assured them I was without much detail. The third week I was out, there were training classes for a few hundred people to let them know that I would return in a few weeks as a woman named Grace Stevens, and that I might look a bit different. I shared some of this story in my memoir, *No! Maybe? Yes! Living My Truth.*

I was overwhelmed by the fact that I actually did it. I transitioned my gender. I was now living full-time as the woman I knew I was. Of course, this was not an easy journey, and I had no idea where it would lead me. I had no idea who would accept me, or who may reject me. I had no idea what people would say to me to my face and behind my back. It took me a little while to realize I did not really know this before I transitioned either.

I was euphoric, in that I was expressing the woman within me the only way I knew how—with clothes, hair, and makeup. Each day was a fashion show for my coworkers. However, almost everyone said that Grace was very different than Larnie used to be. Grace always was happy, they said. I learned that this is what they said behind my back. Happy is how I felt, but I had no idea that they could see it.

I knew that transitioning was not all about the clothes, the hair, and the makeup, but I think that those of us who take this step function path of transitioning will go through this part of our journey. As my days of living my truth continued, I wondered who I—who Grace really was. What do I believe in? What do I stand for? Now that I am no longer hiding from the world, do I have a voice that defines who I am? There were still so many voices inside me who were there for so many decades. Some were quite vocal and some watched all that time in silence. Many of these voices had a chance to express their thoughts and feelings which I shared in my memoir, but there were many more voices. I came to understand that the act of changing my gender was far from the end of this journey.

Some people are adamant that the event of gender transition is the hardest journey anyone could ever take. Even if I thought this way for a moment, I struggle with generalizing these journeys, as I could only speak for my own experience. I knew how hard it was for me to make the decision to transition, but the actual act was an adventure, not a burden.

I did not even know my own real voice. I knew I was living aligned as the woman I am, but I knew there was discovery work to do. I have learned to be patient. I think that transitioning at age 64 testifies to that. I was beginning to understand that all those voices, all those internal debates, were all parts of me but no single one of them defined me. I knew what the next set of tasks was going to be all about. I needed to find my voice. I was living my truth, as my true gender, but I still needed to find and speak from my true voice.

True Colors

I see your true colors
And that's why I love you
So don't be afraid to let them show
Your true colors
True colors are beautiful
Like a rainbow

– Lyrics by John Kenneth Wetton, Geoff Downes

It was Thursday, April 28, 2011. My facial feminization surgery marked my transition to live as my true, authentic self. There were so many unknowns ahead of me. I felt a sense of peace, mixed with amazement that I took that step without knowing anything about where the journey would lead me. By Friday night I was home, back in my own bed to recuperate for the next four weeks. I was now Grace Stevens 24/7. Between the pain-killing narcotics those first few days, I knew I needed to learn who Grace really was. The inner voices telling me I was not living my truth quieted down, but there was another voice or two asking, "Who are you really?" I needed to figure out how to answer this question. The only way was to take one step at a time.

I was bandaged and black and blue for weeks, as I recovered and worked through my next steps. In the picture below, you can see my recovery from day 4, 10, 21, and 28 post surgery.

I had a friend who once asked the question (and not the joke version) of what is the difference between a cross-dresser and a transsexual? The answer was that a cross-dresser gets dressed up and a transsexual gets dressed. I had a lot of women's clothes overflowing my closets. Every piece was meticulously picked out, and I used to obsess as to when and where I would wear them. I can still find the files both in print and digitally of me in each and every piece of woman's clothing I owned.

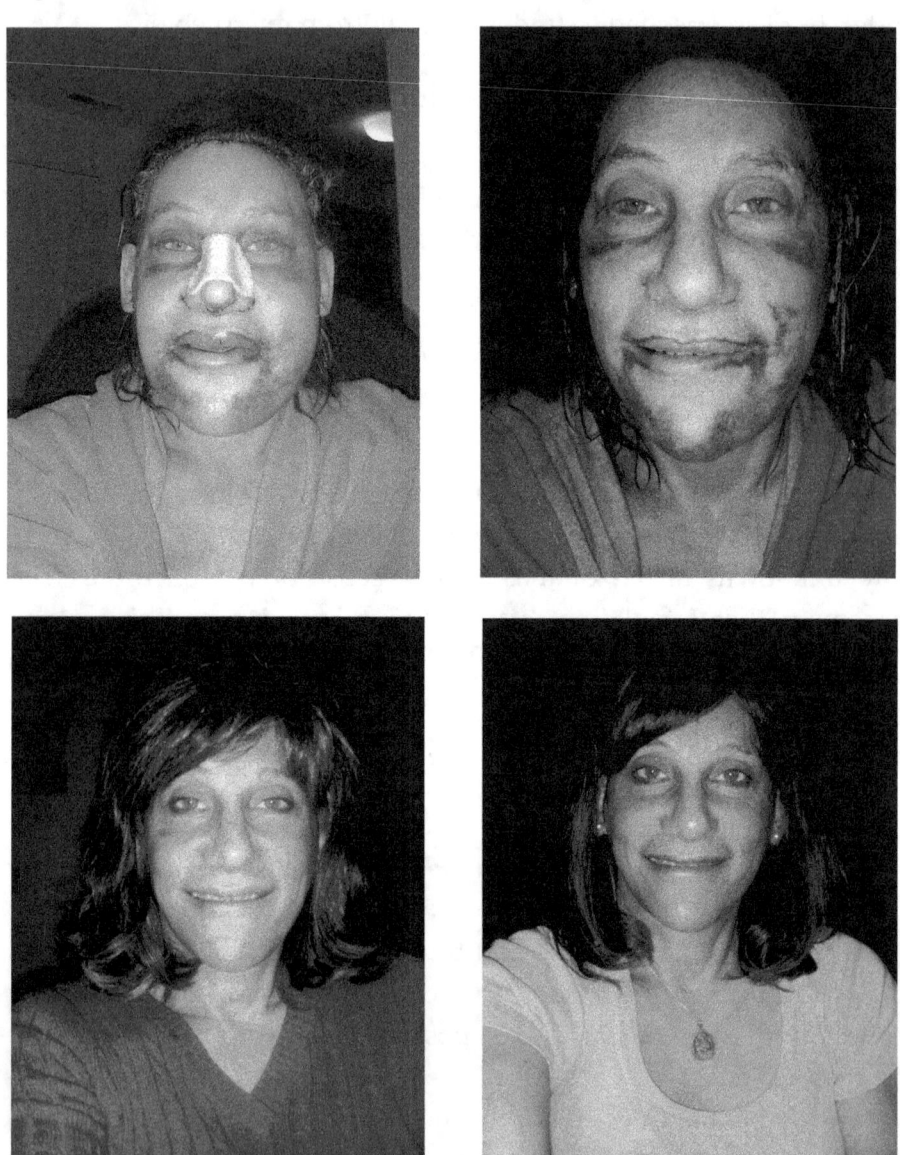

Facial feminzation surgery recovery.

However, I was not quite ready to understand what everyday life, working in two jobs, days and evenings, would be like for Grace—now the 24/7 Grace! I had no idea how I would dress when I returned to work. I needed to do something. I did! A friend had recommended an image consultant to me who had helped her when she had transitioned. I called and made an appointment and was so pleasantly surprised by this adventure. I went to see Ginger Burr of Total Image Consultants (http://totalimageconsultants.com).

I had the most marvelous experience as Ginger evaluated my colors (I had no idea about this process) and interviewed me to get a sense of who I was—which was what I was wanting to know myself—and then also helped me select the proper makeup and gave me lessons on how to apply it. As part of the package I ordered, a week later she joined me on a two-hour shopping session where she was my personal stylist/shopper, and helped me buy a completely new wardrobe. I have no idea how I would have gone back to work without her help.

Grace's color pallette and spirit.

Of all the amazing experiences with her, when I received my color palette, I was floored when I saw the card that captured what she called my "mood." The words that she felt defined me—Grace. Here it is:

Blissfully authentic; carefree; radiant; gracious; soulful

I was only a few weeks into my new life, and Ginger was the first new person that I, as Grace, had contact with. She saw me as blissfully authentic. Perhaps this was the right path for me. At that time, I had no idea that I would become a writer and teacher, about living authentically. I could barely see past my nose (the new, smaller one, that is!) I thought about this experience a lot. I am certain this was the beginning of my musings on living authentically.

I owned a great deal of clothes that did not match my palette, I needed to purge from my "dressing up" days, as I slowly learned that each day I could find my true colors and just get dressed.

Finding My Voice

Give voice to what you know to be true, and do not be afraid of being disliked or exiled. I think that's the hard work of standing up for what you see.

– Eve Ensler

Fear is present in every choice we make in our lives. Humans are social animals. We need to belong to something; we need attachment to a group, a tribe, perhaps a religion. This is innate in our very being. However, the group that we are a member of, whether it was as simple as being born into a group, or more complicated in that we chose it, will help define the ways and accepted values for those who belong. We often fear the conflict when we struggle with these values that do not represent our true feelings and voice, and the threat of being abandoned, disconnected, or even exiled from the group. How often do we choose to silence our voice both internally and externally, in order to keep the connections we are programmed to need?

For those of us who are transgender, it is often a challenging path to at first discover that there is nothing wrong with us for being who we are, and then making some hard choices to do something about it. I have said before that no two journeys will be the same. My sense is that people in and outside of the trans community may have some familiarity with this concept, but still would like to understand who we are in a simple manner. It seems to me that each person who is trans and transitions may feel they are an expert on the transgender experience, and many will find an audience to learn from them. Certainly there are some commonalties between experiences within the trans community, but the more people I meet in my own journey continues to convince me how individual each of our stories are. Pretty much like any other group, there are differences of opinions, arguments, and fights over what people say and believe.

I knew I needed to have my own experience, not anyone else's. I learned to listen to everyone's story. I learned that I had to write my own unique story.

I needed to find my voice. Did I have a voice that was independent of the internal struggle that was there for decades? Could I make friends? I had no idea what that would entail as so many of my parts would push people away to protect my secret. I was tired of hiding who I was, but did I need to stand up and announce myself as transgender? Even now as a somewhat public and perhaps "professional" trans person, I still ask this question.

I started to take improvisation classes, primarily to find Grace's voice. This helped and led to the story that began my book *No! Maybe? Yes! Living My Truth.* I was open in answering questions both within and outside of the transgender community.

I started a training company on gender variance and was well received. I realized that I had more passion in talking about living authentically than gender or transgender rights. The more I thought about it, the more I would talk and then write, which convinced me this was work that I had to do. Some would call it an obsession, sometimes I think of it as a mission, but in either case I know it is my passion. My years in facilitating psycho-education groups helped me learn the skills of talking extemporaneously and creatively while still teaching. I would like to think I am a natural, but no, I experienced the decades of hiding. My first time in front of a large group, I was panicked. Not so much anymore. These were learned skills. I, Grace, discovered her voice, and that I can talk about many topics. I discovered that I could listen and I could teach. I discovered that I loved it. Then I discovered that I could also write. I, who over 40 years ago was trained as an engineer and never took an English class in college, could write. I am amazed, and have no clue where it comes from—but it doesn't matter. No, not at all!

My Fingers Can Speak

It took me quite a long time to develop a voice,
and now that I have it, I am not going to be silent.

– Madeleine Albright

The old engineer in me wanted to control everything. It came as quite a surprise that I wrote my first book of about fifty thousand words in approximately six weeks by letting go of control. All the ideas that were in my mind, some only fragments and some full paragraphs, never made it onto the page as my mind's eye said them.

I would sit by my computer and as my fingers reached out to the keyboard, I experienced the magic. The words and sentences that appeared on my screen often surprised me, as I had a part of myself observing the entire process. I often think of myself as a conduit. My fingers are connected to somewhere either inside or outside of me. I have accepted that it really does not matter to me as I watch them speak and just enjoy being part of the process. I know some people need to plan and write an outline. I am one of those who work from a title or a thought, and just step back. If nothing flows I walk away for another time, without any anger or disappointment. I learned to trust when it occurs or does not occur. Luckily wherever this comes from, I know about deadlines, when they exist, and deal with it in my unconscious mind.

Perhaps there will be a day when my fingers will forget how to speak. I will be OK with that should it occur. It has been fascinating to be part of this journey, in so many ways.

Muses and Musings

I have been blessed to have a few people I consider to be muses in my life. One inspired me to return to school and learn counseling, one inspired me to live my truth, and another inspired me to write my first book.

---

muse [\ ˈmyüz \ -]

As a verb, to muse is to consider something thoughtfully. As a noun, it means a person — especially a woman — who is a source of artistic inspiration.

Vocabulary.com

After my first book, I learned to allow the musings in my mind to be written down. Week after week, I waited for a thought, an idea to form and become a musing. First my mind captured a title, and then I let my fingers speak.

This collection of my musings from 2015 has no single agenda. They are the random wanderings of my mind week by week. I hope that as you proceed along the random paths I followed, you have as much enjoyment reading them as I did in writing them. They are listed chronologically here, but you can pick any one in any order to read. I hope that it makes no difference whether you are trans or not, that you will find a small seed of inspiration to help you consider to perhaps change ever so slightly and move onto a path to live authentically.

My Missionary Positions

"Nothing that I can do will change the structure of the universe.
But maybe, by raising my voice I can help the greatest of all causes—goodwill among men and peace on earth."

– Albert Einstein

I keep telling myself that there is some reason I have created all of these little stories. I recently printed out this bitmoji that sums it up for me. I have received the occasional call and message of thank you for what I have written. I have learned and totally accept that someone can make the world a better place one person at a time. I actually like this missionary position.

I hope that you enjoy my stories and that one or more may inspire you also to make the world a better place.

Bereishit: In the Beginning

I transitioned in April 2011. I cannot remember how the call came, but I was asked to write a guest blog for Bay Windows. I had never done this before, and of course, writing for the blog meant I would be publically announcing that I am transgender. Back then, it seemed that when trans people wrote, it was always about trans rights. My first experience was no different. It took a number of years before I wrote again. By that time, I found a different voice and had lots to write about. In the beginning, it was a political statement about rights. I wrote about "The Meaning of Courage—and Why Lawmakers Need to Show Some Now." Even now, many years later, I think it is still accurate.

Posted (in Bay Windows): 09/2011

The Meaning of Courage—
And Why Lawmakers Need to Show Some Now

1960: I am 13 years old. Puberty is well underway, and I dress in my mother's clothes whenever I'm alone in the house. My seventh-grade social studies class at PS99 in Brooklyn is assigned to read *Profiles in Courage* by John F Kennedy. Reading about acts of courage is inspiring, but I doubt I'll ever be able to act on what is right and true for me. I am very confused.

2003: I am 55 years old. My marriage of 25 years is over and my kids are adults who are leading their own lives. I live alone and dress in women's clothes every evening after work. I somehow find the courage to tearfully confide my secret to a friend. Though I fear losing her friendship, her casual response—"Whatever floats your boat!"—is unexpected and relieves me. Still, I am very confused.

2008: I am 61 years old and several years into a master's degree program at Lesley University. I cannot deny that my choice of study is motivated, in part, to help me understand myself more than others—but that is another story entirely. During my third year of classes, I sign up for Counseling LGBT Clients. During that class I present on the topic of male-to-female transgender identity. The presentation marks my coming out as transgender. My personal act of courage is met with support and acceptance by my classmates. But I am plagued with doubts about what I should do next. Do I continue as I am or begin to transition? I still feel deep shame about who I am. I find the Tiffany Club of New England and meet other people like myself who are just coming out. I meet long-time cross-dressers, transsexuals, and their partners. I am amazed, overwhelmed—and, if possible, even more confused than ever.

2009: I am 62 years old. I have found others like myself. I have dressed as a woman in public. I have come out to my ex-wife and my children. I am an activist in the trans community, and I am working hard at leaving the shame I still feel behind. I still feel confused.

2010: I am 63 years old. I have decided to take hormones and let my hair grow. I schedule facial surgery in preparation for living full-time as a woman. I inform my employer of what's happening and to-gether we plan how to make my transition successful at work. I am—at long last—beginning to feel less confused.

2011: I am 64 years old. In March, I legally change my name to Grace Anne Stevens. In April, I undergo nine hours of facial surgery. In May, I obtain a new driver's license identifying me as female. In Ju-ly, I receive a new passport also identifying me as female. Over two hundred people at work attend informational classes on what I am do-ing and why people transition. When I return to work, I am fully ac-cepted and supported by everyone. I am struck by the consistency of the comments nearly everyone makes: "You are so brave, you are so courageous!" Even if they do not understand it, they still comment on my courage!

So, what is courage? How is it that by being truthful and choosing to live as the person I am born to be make me courageous? I think the best answer can be found in Brene Brown's book, *I Thought It Was Just Me (But It Isn't)*, as she explains that one of the earliest meanings of the word "courage" was "To speak one's mind by telling one's heart." I'd like to see lawmakers show some courage by passing the Transgender Equal Rights Bill. It won't take nearly as much courage as that shown by people who live openly transgender. They do not appreciate why we need protection from discrimination in public places, at work, and in schools. But Kennedy's *Profiles in Courage* tells the stories of eight Senators who showed courage. Two were from Massachusetts, where we have a long history of doing the right thing.

Each person who is transgender must find their truth and have the courage to speak it and live it no matter how others may perceive it. In our democracy, each person is declared to be equal, yet in our system this means "everyone."

So let's see some courage. Pass the Transgender Equal Rights Bill.

Transitioning at Age 64

I had no idea that this blog would be the first of many. I had recently published my book and was pinching myself that I was accepted as a blogger on Huffington Post. I had no idea if I would ever write another. I had no idea that My Transgender Life *would become a brand. Yes it is true—every journey starts with a single step.*

Posted: 02/06/2015

It was another snowy Friday morning, and I met my son and eight-month-old grandson at the mall. I always treasure these walks on the rainy, cold, or snowy days when we can chat about almost anything.

My son started telling me that the afternoon before, he had ESPN radio on in the background, as he is a stay-at-home Dad taking care of the eight-month-old *and* his three-year-old sister. He said he had heard the guys on the radio talking about the latest stories about Bruce Jenner possibly transitioning genders at the age of 65. He said that, normally, he would have ignored it, except for the fact that I, his father, am a transgender woman. He went on about the guys on the radio ranting about not understanding how, or why, a 65-year-old man would ever want to become a woman. Since I transitioned at the age of 64, I told my son that instead of whining that they didn't understand — why didn't they try to find out?

My son responded to me that even though I transitioned, and he accepts me completely, there are still so many things about transgender people that he does not understand. I know he is not alone, so perhaps I can help.

My name is Grace Anne Stevens, and even one decade ago, I did not have the words to understand all the deep feelings inside of me that kept fighting the outward reality that I was a man. I was in my mid-fifties, and had three adult children trying to figure out their own lives, while I—the loving and supportive father—was battling a personal turmoil that no one could see. I was divorced and on my own after 25 years of marriage, and at the age of 58, returned to school to get my master's degree in counseling psychology. Four years later, at age 62, I graduated having learned, among other things, that many of my classmates were trying to figure themselves out, too.

This was a crucial time for me. I was finally able to come to terms with the reality that I was transgender, in fact, transsexual, and made my decision to transition. Not only did I find community, but I became a leader in the community. Over the past six years, I've met and become a trusted resource of hope and knowledge for many people on similar journeys, but that was not my only transition. I no longer work full-time in the engineering field. I now work as a mental health clinician in a substance abuse clinic. I do transition training in the corporate world and speak in schools. My work is dedicated to increasing transgender awareness, and helping others to support those in their groups who transition.

You'd be surprised by how busy I am. I devote many hours trying to find the words to help people understand what they don't know about the transgender journey. As a transgender woman, father, mental health counselor and author, I've devoted myself to shedding light on what it's like to come out as transgender. My book, *No! Maybe? Yes! Living My Truth*, is my story. I wrote it to defy the conventional wisdom that roots transitioning in secrecy and shame. The reality is confusing, and the words, for anyone, are hard to find. But those words must be found, because the decision to transition deserves understanding and respect.

So, that brings me to Bruce Jenner. We don't know, but if the reports are, in fact, true, his own journey will be unique to him as mine was to me. I know it was challenging enough for me at age 64 to transition as a private person. For Jenner, a famous and beloved Olympic athlete living in the very public and over-exposed world of the Kardashians, we can only imagine his challenges. So, for those tempted to feed off of what will surely be sensationalized speculation, I offer three points of firsthand knowledge to help understand being transgender:

o   Sex is not the same as gender: Sex refers to biology and anatomy, while gender is both a psychological sense of self, and a set of cultural defined norms that are expected to be adhered to.

o   Being transgender is not a choice: We are just beginning to understand that, like sexual orientation, our gender identity is pre-wired in our brains.

o   Transgender people have appeared in all cultures throughout our history, with some cultures accepting and honoring them and others rejecting them.

In our culture, the typical norm is: sex = gender = sexual orientation. When one is young and realizes their sense of self does not fit the norm, they often go in to hiding, and they find ways to overcompensate to keep their secret. The fear of not belonging and abandonment overshadow the inner need to be authentic. However, for many people, the hiding cannot last forever.

Most are often surprised, or even shocked to hear of someone transitioning gender in their fifties, sixties, seventies or even eighties. What we see is just the tip of the iceberg, not the lifelong internal struggle, or the decades of hiding and denial, or the lying to oneself about an unquestionable personal reality. We must go deep enough to understand, because only then can we have compassion for a transgender person who has been carrying such a heavy burden in isolation for so long.

What people often don't see is that for many transgender people the act of coming out and transitioning means to realize the loss of everyone and everything achieved in life, knowing you cannot go on living a lie. Living your authentic life after the years of hiding is a conscious decision. Knowing that to become visible is to accept your personal truth, because it outweighs the risk of losing what until now has mattered most in life. Understanding this affirmation is crucial.

Reality is that, too often, editorial decisions are made to debate personal choices on the national stage. The game is to generate heat, not light, so the transgender conversation typically begins and ends with: "I don't understand." There is no acknowledgement of how difficult it is to make the choice to live as one's authentic self. I can only hope that by telling my story, I can help shape an informative conversation grounded in knowledge and compassion. Our words have power, and when we find the right ones, understanding might not be so difficult. Let that be our goal.

Living Your True Life: What Everyone Can Learn from the LGBT Community

I suddenly had delusions that I was a writer. I believed that what I had to say was important and after the acceptance of the initial blog, I wondered whether I could write another that would be published. I really did not know how it worked—not that I do now! My second attempt was published a week later, but received very few likes, especially compared to the first. I wondered if I already lost my way.

Posted: 02/17/2015

I always loved their uniforms.

The tall, black, furry hats; the bright red jackets; the red pinstripe down the legs of the black trousers.

Guards at Buckinham Palace.

Most of all, I loved that no one, no matter how hard they tried, could change the expression on their faces. I am sure that you have seen them so many times. These are the guards at Buckingham Palace.

There were parts of me that acted just like them, guarding the palace that was me! They were on duty 24 hours a day, 365 days a year and would do anything to protect me and my secrets. No one could make them budge, make them smile, or make them laugh. They knew what their job was and they did it well. They kept people away from me. They never complained, and for over 60 years they never let me know how tired they were of doing this job. They were very good at their job that they thought was protecting me.

Although deep inside I knew what they were protecting me from, it took many decades before I accepted that they were protecting me not from others, but really from my own truth.

The truth that I am transgender.

Once I accepted this—my truth—and decided to do something about it, my palace guards were allowed to step down and find other jobs. The details of my story and how it might help you can be found in my memoir, *No! Maybe? Yes! Living My Truth*.

I have this sense that everyone has some form of their own palace guards—protecting some aspect of their own truth that they hope others never ever will discover. Being protective is a basic truth of being human, to be attached to the herd, to be a member and conform to one group or another. Yet, another facet is that each and every one of us is an individual and has our own unique thoughts and desires that we think that if we expressed or acted on them, we would be banished from the herd.

In our culture, when our uniqueness touches the areas of sexual orientation or gender identity, these seem to be such great triggers for the society at large to say, "No! You are not like us, and we will send you out of the herd, the tribe. We do not like, do not accept your difference, your uniqueness. You threaten us, and our way of living. We cannot tell you why, but you do!"

I am astonished that in the past few days we have seen a vivid example of xenophobia in the public arena. The governor of Kansas, Sam Brownback recently rescinded a seven-year-old executive order that provided job protection for LGBT state employees. In a country founded on the principles of all men are created equal and entitled to life, liberty, and the pursuit of happiness, how can such an event occur? A governor makes a statement that a specific group of people who were once protected is no longer protected. Your rights have been taken away. Effectively, the message is you are no longer equal to the rest of us—we are afraid of you and do not like you and perhaps do not want you in our herd. I am not sure that astonishment is even the right word!

A few quotes come immediately to my mind. The first is from George Santayana:

> *Those who cannot remember the past are condemned to repeat it.*

And then, the famous message from Martin Niemoeller, a Lutheran pastor regarding living in World War II Germany:

> *They first came for the Communists,*
> *and I didn't speak up because I wasn't a Communist.*
> *They then came for the Jews,*
> *and I didn't speak up because I wasn't a Jew.*
> *They then came for the trade unionists,*
> *and I didn't speak up because I wasn't a trade unionist.*
> *Then they came for the Catholics,*
> *and I didn't speak up because I was a Protestant.*
> *Then they came for me,*
> *and by that time no one was left to speak up."*

When will we all recognize that as human beings, we are all part of the same herd? Our challenge is to find the balance to be who we are and also be part of the greater community—the herd. It is time that we move from a place of fear of those who are different to recognize that those who may be different may have something to teach us all.

We in the LGBT community know that our inner lives have improved when our own guards have retired, and wonder what it might take for others to stop living in fear of not only our truth, but also their own truth. We wonder!

The freedom of being yourself and following your inner voice, your inner truth, is personal freedom and priceless. For people in the LGBT community, the journey to live their truth is often filled with both internal and external battles to achieve personal freedom. How can this choice be wrong? How can this decision harm others? Isn't the freedom to be yourself what we all strive for—even if our own guards are blocking it?

I believe that everyone should be able to live their own true life. When we talk about "people like us," let's stop looking as to whether they are black or white, red or yellow, gay or straight, or transgender. Why don't we look for, and make "people who express their truth" the most important criteria of the herd we wish to belong to?

Within the LGBT community, so many of us have come through the battles to live our truth. We have let our palace guards retire, even if we loved the uniforms. Perhaps we can be the teachers to so many others that it is OK to live your authentic lives. Are you ready to let your guards retire, too? Everyone can learn a lesson from us.

Hard Choices That Were Not Only Mine

My publicist kept telling me the media wants conflict. I kept resisting, even as I was discovering and evolving my voice. I thought that the title of the first blog, My Transgender Life, *might even be a brand. I still did not have a full sense of my voice, or that I was becoming a storyteller, but I sensed it was getting clearer. I even added my son's voice in this posting. I believe that his voice is the one that can truly change the world.*

Posted: 02/24/2015

I would not dare utter the word!

It was like the characters in the Harry Potter books who were afraid to utter the name Voldemort out loud. Just thinking about it was scary enough, but saying the name out loud would be certain to bring impending doom.

Yes, it was just like that.

This was five years ago, and I had already, a year earlier in 2009, come out to my family and neighbors that I was transgender and cross-dressed to go out as a woman.

Telling them was hard, but not the hardest choice I had to make.

Sometime in the middle of 2010 I began to understand that I was not a cross-dresser. I was a…a….a…

I was 63 years old and never could say the word out loud. I was afraid that if I dared to utter it—if the word formed and left my lips, it would make it true—and then—my life would be over. Deep down I knew it was true, I did, and I knew it for a long, long time.

I finally summoned all the courage within me, accepted my truth and said the word. I am a ...a...a...transsexual.

Telling myself this truth was hard, but not the hardest choice I had to make.

Now that I reached the point of self-acceptance, the question at hand was whether or not I would transition and live the rest of my life as my true self. What if my kids could not handle their father becoming a woman? What if? If I chose my own path and journey, would that be selfish? If they abandoned me, could I deal with it? I had no idea how they would take it, and I heard so many stories of bad outcomes from people who had traveled this path before.

This was my hardest choice. My kids were all adults at this time and I was living on my own for the past nine years after a twenty-five-year marriage. I told myself I had to move forward. If my kids could not deal with it, that was not under my control or even my responsibly. Perhaps this decision was selfish, or wrong, but it was the hardest choice I ever made.

This was the decision to move forward even in the face of potential losses.

I have been one of the lucky ones. I have been blessed in that I went forward and have lost no one in my family. I know that many people have not had this experience. When we choose to go on our own journey of truth, we will force those closest to us in life to go a journey that they were most likely not expecting, and not wanting to take. I realized how hard it was for me to wrestle with my choices, but it was even harder for me to put myself in my kid's shoes to understand what must be going through their minds and hearts. I just wanted their acceptance first. If I was lucky, perhaps they would also understand. I did not realize how hard this latter part might be. I transitioned in 2011, and last year as I was writing my book, one of my sons and his wife shared what their experience of my journey was like for them.

In my book, *No! Maybe? Yes! Living my Truth,* I shared that conversation I had with my son Elie and his wife, Becca. They told me how it was for them when I shared that I was transgender (I was 62 at the time). I was in Boston and they were in Tucson, so we had a long conversation over the phone. They were totally supportive. Here's a bit of what we said:

Becca: Elie talked to you a long time and I was hoping everything was OK. He came in and told me that everything was OK, but my dad just told me he was transgender. I said, "Oh! That's a surprise." Usually when there is a long conversation it is terrible news.

Grace: For some, many people this would be terrible news.

Elie: Right, for many people that would be terrible news...but what I feel like it is just news...

Becca: Surprising news.

Elie: Just a turn of events. Sexual identity, gender identity, those are just who you are. Like if you called and said you were gay, or are gay, then it would have been like, OK to me, it didn't have a big...well, it did have a big effect on me, but it doesn't directly change who I am...or change what my relationship with you is.

During the conversation, I asked them if my transition caused them any losses. Elie told me that he lost the illusion that his dad always had a happy life.

Elie: I need my life not to be living like that. My dad has been unhappy for 60 years; we need to make sure we don't do that. We always make sure we are living the life we want to live.

It appears that by choosing the path to live my truth, my son was inspired to make sure he lives his!

Later in the conversation Elie made the most important statement:

Elie: I don't understand why I would cut you off. I don't understand any situation where a parent would abandon a kid or a kid would abandon a parent. I don't understand how to do anything different but care for you, because you cared for me forever. We all care for each other, and you didn't do anything wrong...

These are the family values that are important. Love and acceptance, and the realization that when you live your truth and just be who you really are—*you have not done anything wrong.*

Yes, I have been very blessed. After decades of wrestling with myself thinking I was doing something wrong, or even worse, that I was wrong, now I know—*I have done nothing wrong!* I could not utter those words until my son said them out loud. These are powerful words. Far more powerful than words that bring the feelings of impending doom, these words bring everlasting joy.

The hard choices of my journey were not only mine. They were hard choices for my family too, and I am thankful for the choices they made. We will always be a family.

Reality is that our journey to living our truth is not always easy. Our hard choices often force others to make hard choices. We can only hope that the map for making these choices has a legend guided by love, compassion, and understanding.

(The full conversation between Grace and her son can be found in her book, *No! Maybe? Yes! Living My Truth*)

Where Is God?

Three weeks in a row on Huffington Post. *Something changed in me. At first it was all about getting my name out in order to sell books. I still do not know how, but from somewhere inside, there were stories brewing and percolating into my mind and then escaping through my fingers on the keyboard. I questioned these at first, but over time I have learned to ride them and see where they take me. This post crossed over from the Gay Voices pages into the Religion pages, and I received feedback from far and wide—and made new contacts and friends. This was an unexpected new path on my journey.*

Posted: 03/04/2015

I am not a religious person. There! I said it.

My parents were not religious either. They were first-generation Americans born in 1914 and 1918 and grew up during the Great Depression struggling to get by in Brooklyn, New York.

I am a baby boomer, born in 1947, and have no idea what life must have been like for them. I have no idea of struggling to get by. As a child, I had no idea I was not religious, because it was never present in my household—there were no rituals, and therefore, I was never programmed to have a sense of God and needing to follow some set of religious rules.

I was raised in the fifties and sixties and pretty much learned right from wrong by watching the early days of TV. Cowboys and Indians defined the good guys and the bad guys, right from wrong. It took many years to realize my programming was faulty.

In 1960, I was 13 and Bar Mitzvahed like all my friends in the neighborhood. This is the coming-of-age ritual for Jewish boys when they get to say, "Today I am a man!" Even at such a young age I knew this was a lie, but I dared not let anyone else know. I was already thoroughly in hiding and knew deep inside being a man was the furthest thing from my truth.

Fast forward: When it was time to send my children to Hebrew School, the rabbi thought I should go for conversion lessons, as I had no knowledge or sense of my religious heritage. I declined. I was still deeply hiding.

Fast forward: In 2011, I transitioned my gender, and got to say, "Today I am a woman!" This felt right and true, and freed me from hiding. Now there was so much reprogramming to do.

I am still not a religious person, but I know my life's journey has been full of blessings. I have no other words or way to articulate how I feel, so this brings me to my view of God.

I see God as a force for good...like a good parent, providing me guidelines of right and wrong and sending me out in the world to live my life and find my truth. God does not micromanage me and tell me what to do in every moment. The gift of life came with the basic program called free will, and I must choose the best path to travel. Even when I face tough challenges or receive blessings that often come in very mysterious ways, free will calls me to make my own choices. Through the years I have learned it is much better to choose the path of love over the path of fear.

I see a loving God, not a wrathful God. I see a forgiving God and not a punishing God.

It seems to me that if you believe in a wrathful God, you follow a path of fear and spend far too much time living in a place of hate. I never want to be in that place, yet many people are, and since writing about my transgender life, I've felt that hate firsthand. Right here, after my first blog appeared, there were people who responded with a terrible lack of compassion and understanding of my journey to live my truth. This negativity came from a place of hate. One person seemed to have more compassion for animals than sensitivity for people who might be different than him. He condemned me for my choices in one breath, and in another proclaimed tenderhearted compassion for rescue animals in a series of posts on his Facebook page. He obviously reconciled the two. I may love animals too, but can't reconcile it like that.

The truth is that we are all different in some manner. In my teaching, I often say we are like snowflakes in that each of us is unique. I kept that in mind when I read those hateful comments. Yes, I was hurt for the moment, but I was more sad than hurt. Really, it was the others who chose to defend what I had written who restored my faith. I still only see a loving God.

I will never understand how, in the name of religion, people can allow themselves to discriminate against LGBT people and then work to make that discrimination legal. I always thought that the Golden Rule, "Treat others as you would like them to treat you," appeared prominently in many religions to teach us the definition of right and wrong.

Discrimination in any form does not come from a loving God, or a loving person. Discrimination occurs when people travel the path of fear. This path is not freeing, it is confining. It hurts both internally and externally. I know this from the decades of hiding my own truth and living in shame and fear of discovery.

My journey has taught me that being true to oneself is the only way to be free. Change is not easy, but it is possible. Acceptance, with or without full understanding, comes when we choose the path of love over the path of fear. We've all must choose the path we travel. My choice saved me and gave me the life I dreamed of living. If you are waiting to face your truth, turn away from the path of fear. Take the path of love. You'll be amazed to see what blessings await you.

When I Was a Young Girl

I was watching TV, and there was a character who said, "When I was a young girl...." It was like a seed planted just below my consciousness. The next morning was the first time I had to rush to my computer and capture this story while I still could remember it. The first line describes so much of my life now.

Posted: 03/10/2015

When I was a young girl.

Memory is a funny thing.

I think I am one of the lucky ones as I get to travel down so many memory lanes.

There are so many memories of my inner world that no one ever was privy to. There are also all the memories of my external world, growing up, going to school, getting married, raising a family.

There are also the more recent memories of realizing these two worlds were both real and could come together in alignment. In my personal experience, parallel lines, or parallel lives, can and do meet and can become a single line or life. I am so much better for this.

— ☼ —

When I was a young girl, no one ever knew I was there. I was invisible. I was so quiet, so silent, and I dared not let anyone see me or hear me. I was watching everything and waiting and dreaming for the day when it might be safe to come out. It was very hard, each and every day for me, and I knew I was alone. There were so many days when I would hide, but every now and then, I did peek out at the world. But I dared not let anyone see me.

When I was a young girl, I watched the other young girls. I wanted to play with them, but there was no way I could take the chance. What would they say? What would everyone say if I took that risk? After all, they did not see me. How could they? All they saw was the young boy that was in control of this body we shared. He was in here too, in the inner world we shared, but only he got to play in the outer world. We often fought, but he always won, for such a long time. I was not a happy girl!

When I was a young girl, I could dream of anything. I dreamed of flying off to magical places where I could play with the other girls and have friends—yes, most important to have friends who really knew me. Oh! I had so many dreams of friendships. I remember how many times that boy laughed at me and made me feel so badly about myself. I think he was jealous because he never had any friends either.

When I was a young girl, I saw that boy grow up, go to school, and even get married. It was so hard for me to watch, and I spent so much time hiding. When he had kids, I tried to make sure he treated them really well, not the way he treated me. I think I did a good job at this. Even though he was getting older, I was still a young girl, but one that knew so much.

When I was a young girl, I realized I only had one chance left to move to the outer world. I did not want to hurt anyone. I really did not want to hurt those kids who amazingly were now adults themselves. I knew it would not be easy for me. I wondered if they would even want to know me. I wondered if I would at last even find some friends to play with who would really get to know me. I wondered what would happen to that boy — who was already more like an old man.

When I was a young girl, I took the chance!

– ☼ –

Memories are a funny thing. They seem to come and go. Some are always present, and some float in an out of my consciousness randomly. I am pretty sure they are all real! I am still that young girl, and I have made peace with that boy/man who used to be in control of this body. He has so many memories, and we have become friends. He tells me he is happy now, remembering all that happened, and is happy that I am now in charge of this body. He told me he never felt right in it, and he is happy with what I've done to make it mine. So am I, and I told him it fits me perfectly!

He seems to be enjoying what he says are his retirement days, and I laugh with him at this. I am OK when he peeks out and watches what goes on with me, and that he is being really good and lets me stay in control. I know he works very hard at this. He is now one of my friends — and I now have many others.

Sometimes he tells me stories that start with, *"When I was a young boy...."* I am learning to really like these stories.

To the Partners of Those in Transition

By now, I had learned to trust the process and go with the flow. There are a number of later posts where I talk about events that happen at weekly meeting at The Tiffany Club of New England. There were a number of people struggling with the coming-out process with their wives. After a few long nights of back and forth, pros and cons, and mostly primal fears of losing everyone and everything, I had to capture my evolved thoughts on the topic here.

Posted: 03/17/2015

I can't know your pain.

I cannot ever feel or know *your* pain. The pain that someone who may be like me—transgender—has caused. None of us who have been your partners can really understand you, just as it may be hard for you to understand us. All that is clear is that the person you thought you knew appears to be someone very, very different. Perhaps you knew something was up, or perhaps it was a total surprise, but it does not matter. The pain is there, and it is real.

I only know my own pain. That's the pain of confusion, the pain of denial, the pain of suppressing my truth, and the pain of choosing my truth that brings me the pain of maybe losing everyone in my life—even you. But I cannot feel *your* pain. I can only relate to the pain your partner is no doubt experiencing. I suspect those feelings may be much like mine, but we who transition can never know your pain or even find the proper words to apologize for that which we are responsible. No matter how hard we try, we will never know how deeply we may have hurt you.

Perhaps some of you knew about your partner's pain, but could never feel it. How could you? After all, it was not yours. Perhaps you questioned your partner's decision to externally transform. Of course, that transition changed everything for you. For any transgender person, the decision to change is not easy, but it is the only way we can honor our personal truth. It is the decision that frees us to live the life of the person we have always been.

Some of you may have had no idea about your partner's internal struggle. When you learned, I suspect you felt many things, but mostly confused and betrayed. Loss of trust hurts. You may have even thought it was your fault. It was not! And where does love fit into this? Where do all the years of relationship fit? Where is responsibility? Did they mean anything?

When a person decides to transition gender, they force everyone in their life to take a journey also. For many, this is a journey they were not prepared to take, and don't want to take. Once we finally come to our own self-acceptance and choose to change gender, we want everyone to be excited for us, but often neglect to understand the impact on those we are in relationship with.

Are we selfish? We don't see it that way, but I am pretty sure from your viewpoint it looks that way. I understand your reaction but still cannot feel your pain. We see gain where you must see loss. You ask how can we do this to you? Truth is, this choice we've finally made is one of life and death for us, but I doubt that even knowing that can ease your pain. We most likely have burst the bubble of happiness in your life and in return, have asked you to understand and be happy for us. Heartless? Not really. Many of us do not even know how selfish this is and the pain we've caused.

We can and want to share our stories with you, although many of you are hurting so badly you cannot or will not listen. Gender and sexuality topics are difficult enough to deal with even without having a partner decide to change gender mid-relationship. Added to this, no matter how many years we've battled with our internal struggle, we want you to jump on board with us immediately. It hardly ever works this way. I've seen this to be true in both heterosexual and gay/lesbian relationships when one partner transitions. It is an unreasonable request. The transitioning partner will tell you that they are still the same person. My personal and professional view is that when they say that they are still in denial—unaware of where their transition will lead them. What we all come to know is that transition is not a destination. It is just another step on our journey.

And yet, *you* are still in pain, and we are the source.

Even though we know that being transgender is not a choice, we do have a choice of what we do about it. You may even know this, but it does not ease *your* pain.

How often our choice hurts the ones we love most, the ones we care about, the ones we do not want to lose. How often our choice to live our truth results in losing those so dear to us. And yet, we know we must find the courage to make this choice. We have to.

We can't make excuses for the emotional outcome. Many of us don't even know how to articulate our responsibility in a credible manner to you. We often don't know how to ask for your forgiveness, as we will never really understand your pain. We have only just found a way to relieve ours.

No, this is not fair for any of us. Not in any manner!

In his classic book, *The Road Less Traveled,* M. Scott Peck defines love as: "The will to extend one's self for the purpose of nurturing one's own or another's spiritual growth." Each of us can interpret this in our own unique manner. To me, coming to terms with my true gender and making the choice to transition has done so much to nurture my own spiritual growth. It has allowed me to love myself in a way I never could before. I know I have forced those around me to take journeys they did not want to take. My wish for them is that even though there may be pain, they find a path for their own spiritual growth. This is the love I have for them.

Perhaps this perspective is no solace for you, but I hope it is. I cannot feel your pain, but I do know someone's transgender journey may have caused it. We can only hope that in time, through the love that at one time was there, you will find a way to accept that our intention has never been to hurt—only to heal. Maybe then, we will find a way to continue the journey we were destined to make.

Explain It to Me Like I'm a Six-Year-Old

Sometimes I do make things up. But not this one! I heard the three questions that I wrote about in this post at a conference when an experienced therapist shared them with the audience. The more I thought about the concept behind these questions, the more I learned about people's experiences, the more it seemed to be true. I am happy to use it, borrow it, and perhaps reframe it a bit. No matter—it really is accurate.

Posted: 03/24/2015

The mind of a six-year-old. Photo credit: Jamie Taylor.

It all can start with the beginner's mind, *but what is that?*

Think about it. Can you find that six-year-old child still within you? Can you remember when everything new had that *wow!* associated with it and a total lack of judgment?

I am learning to find that part of me once again—although it's a great deal of work.

There once was an innocence, a curiosity, and a willingness to explore. To know, really know, that all I observed was simply that—a discovery. It was not part of me, or said anything about me. I had no judgment, as it was all so new.

I wonder when I lost that. When was innocence replaced with comparisons and judgment? When was willingness to explore replaced by concerns for safety? When was the childlike joy of something new replaced by the stagnation and boredom of responsibility and survival?

Recognizing this change away from innocence and believing the path does not have to be this way has taken time. Each day can be an adventure if you are willing to find your own beginner's mind.

As a transgender woman, it's been fascinating to observe how people respond to coming-out announcements. I've had many opportunities to see what happens when I or others explain their change of gender status. Note, this coming out occurs in different situations for just about everyone. Some are surprised, shocked, curious, or frozen. Some want to talk, and some are silent. Some become closer, and some disappear, never to be seen or heard from again.

However, what amazes me most is to watch the children, the little ones who still operate with a beginner's mind.

A few years ago, I attended a workshop and learned how it is that children truly see the world so differently from adults. For them it's much simpler. They are exploring the world and finding their place in it. Not like us.

When a father who has young children transitions, he is often frozen with fear about how to let them know that daddy is going to be a woman. Children usually respond to what he often sees as a drastic, earth-shattering change that could destroy his family with only three concerns. Their curiosity can be fully satisfied with the right answers to three simple questions:

o   Is it my fault?

o   Do you still love me?

o   Are you going away?

If the answers of no, yes, no respectively come, most six-year-olds will go right back to playing their video games, and all can take a deep breath and move on with what's really important, which you may have heard me say before, taking care of yourself and then the others around you.

I wonder why adults don't look at change the way a six-year-old does. Why can't we explain being transgender to everyone in the same way we would to our children?

Being transgender is no one's fault. Gender identity, like sexual orientation, is just an aspect of who we are and how that quite complicated organ, our brain, is wired.

Being transgender does not change the feelings a parent has for a child, or for anyone with whom they are in relationship. For those who transition gender the only relationship that they change is inside, with themselves, when at long last they can align their body and their mind.

Being transgender does not automatically force the person you know to go away. Most of us who transition desperately don't want to go away, but as we know, all relationships are complicated, and it's not a decision we make alone. I will go on record to emphatically say that it is always better for the children when you don't go away. Sadly, however, for many reasons, that path is not always the one travelled. If only adults would respond with beginner's mind so then they would find the right path.

In the classic book, *Zen Mind, Beginner's Mind,* Shunryu Suzuki states, "In the beginner's mind there are many possibilities, in the expert's mind there are few."

But how do we find our beginner's mind? Ask yourself: Am I willing to look at the world with curiosity, with a sense of adventure, with a willingness to explore without preconceived notions? Am I willing to accept that our culture's preconceived norms of a binary view of gender may not be accurate for all people? Can I accept that it is no one's fault and that there is nothing *wrong* with those who have the courage to change gender? Can I see that they are like me in our mutual need for, and capacity to, give love and compassion and be in relationship? Can I operate from a place of looking for many paths, for many possibilities?

Since I transitioned I wake up and begin each morning with my own version of beginner's mind. In my book I explained it this way:

I awake each morning with no expectations and look forward to the day's adventure."

If you can go deep enough to find your own answers you will understand that explaining gender variance to a six-year-old is not all that hard. It's simply all about love and connection. Children get that. Adults can, too.

I hope you can find your six-year-old child inside and be willing to learn from them, especially about how to live with beginner's mind.

Remember

The following article was rejected twice by the editors at Huffington Post. *Honestly, I was beside myself for so many reasons. The article itself was birthed out of anger from the political situation in Indiana. It was also the time of year nearing Yom Hashoah, the anniversary of remembering the Holocaust. I tried to share my experience, hoping that my voice could and would make a difference. Perhaps because I challenged the powers that be, the post was rejected. I do not know. I shared my experiences, I shared my feelings, and I still would go on the offered trip. There is a part of me that thinks it is even more important now!*

Not Posted: Submitted to Huffinton Post 03/28/2015 but rejected...

"It was the best of times; it was the worst of times."

– Charles Dickens, *Tale of Two Cities*

Dickens first wrote this 156 years ago. For the first time in my life, I know what this feels like.

It is the best of times! It is now four years since I started to live as my true self, and I have been blessed to express, and discover who I am each and every day. I no longer have the inner battle that lasted for six decades and my inner peace is wonderful.

It is the worst of times! I am a baby boomer, born after World War II, and being Jewish grew up with a sense of the Holocaust and what happened before my time. In fact, in 1960, when I turned 13, I purchased my first book, *The Rise and Fall of the Third Reich* by William Shirer. I do not know what drove me to buy that book—perhaps it was an urge stemming from a greater form of universal consciousness, but I remember how difficult it was to understand that Hitler's rise to power could happen. I was so young, and I did not understand. But today, I know much more and have never been as scared as I am to watch what is happening in state after state as they are passing laws under the guise of religious freedom that allows discrimination. Doesn't anyone remember where this systemic discrimination leads?

I am not religious. I am not observant. Yet I am Jewish. Four years ago I also gave up my white male privilege when I transitioned my gender. Now, in Indiana and other states, I may be discriminated against because of someone's religious beliefs. I am trying to remember the lessons I learned growing up about America and wonder where that country is now. I am trying to remember what the *pilgrim's pride* really meant. I do not understand why I am a threat to anyone, when I am finally being true to myself.

Remember.

World War II ended 70 years ago. Does anyone really remember this time? April 15 is Yom HaShoah, the Day of Remembrance. Six million killed! Genocide! The ultimate in discrimination!

Remember.

In 2007 I was on a business trip to Munich. I knew that I would take a side trip to the camp—Dachau. I knew it would be difficult, but I learned so much. So much that I will always remember.

Dachau memorial museum.

The memorial site is a museum. I forced myself to go. It was an inner compulsion that I knew I had to do. I still do not know why, but I am glad that I did.

I did have the expectations to see the camp, the bunks, the gas chambers, and the crematorium. With a heavy, heavy heart I did see all of these things, each so difficult to comprehend how a world where that occurred could exist.

However, I learned that the site serves a purpose. The museum was filled with visiting German school children, all of them had to learn their history—to remember what came before them—to never forget.

Children learning their history at Dachau.

They had step-by-step assignments and reports to fill out. I learned that each child had to learn their history. To be responsible and to never allow it to happen again.

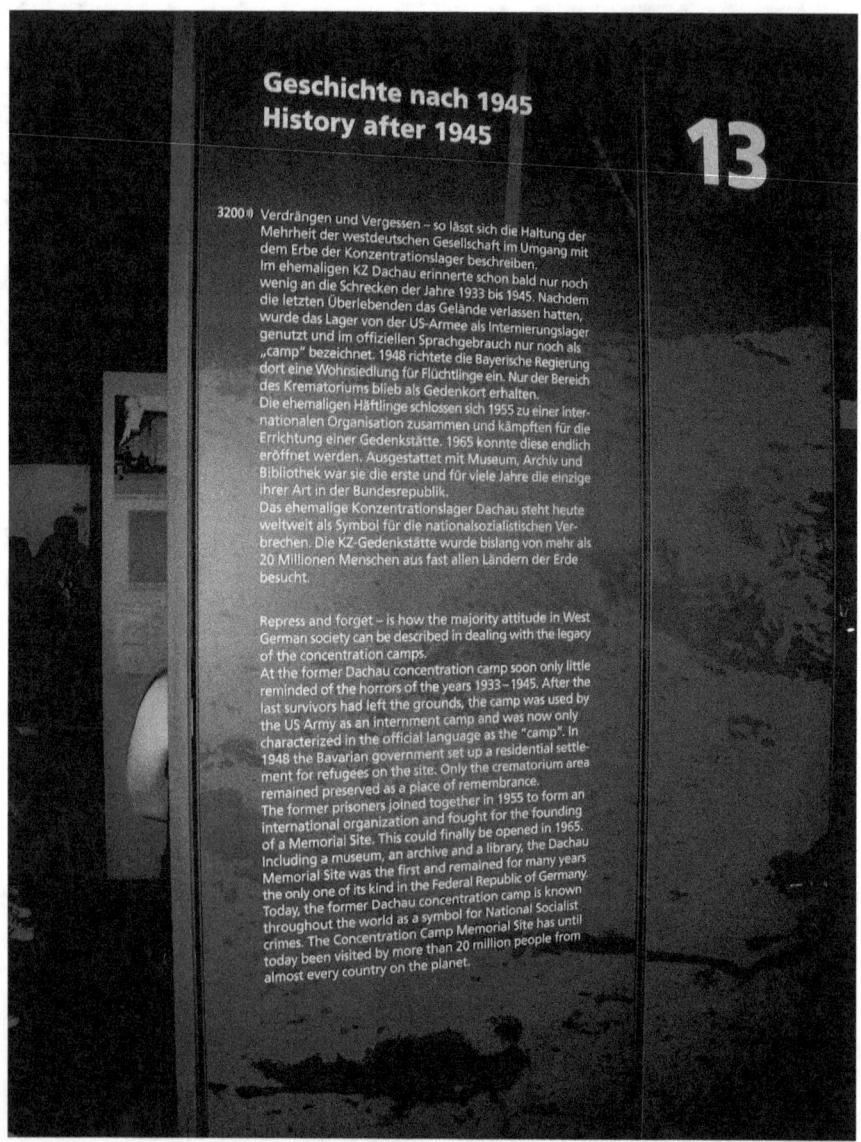

History of Dachau.

– ☼ –

When I was a school child, I remember learning about American history: a country that believed religious freedom meant acceptance and allowance of others no matter how their beliefs might differ. I learned about the challenges of new immigrants and ethnic groups being discriminated against. My teen years paralleled the civil rights movement, yet I was already in hiding to protect my true self. I felt safe for so long. I no longer feel safe, and I don't understand it. However, I am no longer in hiding. No matter how one disguises discrimination and hate, it does not work, it will not work. We who are in the LGBT community are your fathers, your mothers, your sons, your daughters, your cousins, your in-laws, your teachers, your students, your bosses, your customers. We are your neighbors, your pastors, your rabbis. We are just like you, and not a threat to you or your way of life. We are just living ours.

Our country was created by the people who came to escape persecution and discrimination and have the religious freedom to worship as they choose. This has not changed!

For anyone who believes that religious freedom allows one to discriminate against anyone different then you, I invite you to come with me on a trip to camp. To *the* camp, Dachau, and let's do a report together. Let's see if we can remember where the history of discrimination leads. It is not a pretty place, no, not pretty at all.

Perhaps this will be a lesson that can reach your heart, and help you understand where separation and discrimination takes us. For many politicians they are not on the path of love. An apology may not be enough, but if they can begin to understand, we can make things better for all of us. Let's go on a trip. Let's learn together.

We all need to remember what history has taught us! Please! Remember!

Hearts and Minds

I was scrambling. I was worried that since the editors at Huffinton Post had now rejected me, my writing days might be done. I had no idea how they worked. I was angry, and I was scared, and tried to put some of my thoughts together in a less politically polarizing manner. It was a relief when this article was published. I was trying to figure out what lesson was in my experience of the past two weeks. My takeaway was that I am better sharing my own stories than trying to stand on top of a soapbox. If I have any impact, it may be one person at a time. My lesson is that I can accept that as enough!

Posted: 03/31/2015

It took me almost 60 years before I let myself feel anything. I mean *really* feel anything. Perhaps some of you can understand this.

I did not need any kind of drug, or drink to numb myself. To the outside world, I certainly appeared as a fully functional human being. However, inside of me, the ability to care, or share, was held prisoner by the parts of me who feared my truth. I was petrified of not only letting others get to know the real me, but also of getting to know myself.

When asked how I felt about something, I was like a deer in the headlights—frozen. I never knew how to respond. Sure, one part of me or another would always come to the rescue and make up some answer, but I barely heard the words come out of my mouth. Today, I know it was my heart that was frozen. Emotions and feelings were shielded and blocked from either entering or exiting that organ we commonly refer to as the home of love and compassion.

– ☼ –

I have come a long way from that time. My frozen heart has melted, and I have learned to embrace my source of feeling love and compassion. The gentle beating is now the rhythm I march to in my life. For so many decades I hid behind my identity as an engineer and was so proud of my analytical view of just about everything. This identity has now, at last, taken a giant step into the background of my life. My head no longer takes the lead. I've learned that when I let my heart lead in all relationships—with co-workers, with friends, and with loved ones, and yes, even with strangers, I am able to understand things in a new way that is not only so much more satisfying to me, but no longer separates me from others. When I let others in to see the true me, the open me, the vulnerable me, I have a better understanding of relationship. It's not just that I am now clearer about my own feelings; it's that by sharing, I have found a more powerful way to help others understand their own.

Since I began sharing my stories, my feelings, my heart with you in *My Transgender Life* writings, I've heard from so many people. They are getting to know me and have a better understanding of what the journey is like for people like me. I know that being transgender is a difficult concept for many to understand. Sometimes the spouse, or child, or parent who wants to know more has picked up my book and come back to me with questions. They've come to understand that this journey, for all of us, is about so much more that transitioning gender.

In the past few years, as I've been speaking, training, and teaching about gender variance, I have learned so much. When I first started, I had a dozen slides with all the facts about gender transition. I talked about sex and gender and tried to explain what was then called the diagnosis of *gender identity disorder*. My presentation contained so much detail. The audiences were always polite, but when I finally finished my long presentation, I found the questions they asked had nothing to do with the information I'd just presented. Almost every question was about how to talk to someone who was transitioning in the workplace. They wanted to know how to talk to the co-workers they originally knew as a different gender. I realized that their questions came from the heart. They simply wanted to know how to preserve their relationships. They didn't want to offend. They wanted to understand. What if I use the wrong name, or pronoun? Will it be embarrassing if I say he, instead of she by mistake and how do I apologize? If the person goes for surgery, what can I ask? What can they say? Their questions were an eye-opener for me.

I knew how scared I was when I returned to my two different workplaces when I transitioned. Later, with my training and teaching, I realized that so many people were just as scared—maybe even more scared than I had been. They didn't know how to be with a transitioning person. They didn't know what they could say. Their honesty changed me. As this realization moved from my mind to my heart, I began to change the way I teach and talk about the transgender journey. Now, I focus more on feelings. I still share what the life journey looks like, but now I ask about feelings. What's it like when you hear the news of a co-worker's change? How does it feel?

The more I let you into my life, the more I hope you will see how similar our journeys are. My truth was coming to terms with my gender identity and choosing to do something about it at the age of 64. Almost everyone I've met through my training or my book, whether they are transgender or not, has said that my story has helped them to realize that they too have buried, or held back some part of their own truth. They tell me they've cried. I have touched their hearts!

If I can touch your heart, there's a good chance you will begin to understand that those of us who are transgender are just the same as you. We all want to live as authentically as we can. After all, if we can touch your heart, we can change your mind!

Who wants to live their life just to meet the expectations of others? I suspect few want to, yet many do. It is not easy to conquer the fear of following our truth. I know this first hand. It took me too many years to get out of my head and learn to lead with my heart.

I cannot prove it with statistics or any form of analysis, nor do I even try, but I believe if you too, let yourself feel, and operate out of your own heart, and live your own truth, you will not only better understand my journey, but yours as well. You will be living a life of love and compassion.

It is such a better way to live. I believe that with all my heart.

Time Travel Is Not That Hard, But Stopping Is

Pinch me, please! I have always been a dreamer, and even now, there are the moments I am not certain I am in the present moment. For 60 years I have dreamt that I could live my truth. Now that I am, I still have dreams. Sometimes I am not quite certain if they are the old ones being replayed or new ones.

Posted: 04/14/2015

Perhaps it is because I have reached that certain age. What seemed to be well organized and put in their proper time sequence does not seem to work the same way it used to.

More specifically, as I wake up each morning, I am finding I have some confusion separating my memories from my dreams, or is it the other way, my dreams from my memories. Yes, I am very confused as I am starting the day. I am not sure whether I should be worried about this confusion. Now, I did not partake in all those drugs that were around in the sixties and seventies. I swore off weed after a bad experience with some brownies in 1976. I do not drink very much, so I am not melting the myelin sheaths around my axons, so I wonder what is happening to me. Yes, perhaps I have reached that certain age.

— ☼ —

Transitioning my gender four years ago certainly has been an experience of living my dream. Hiding in fear, confusion, and shame for decades ended, and I was released. Learning, or actually relearning, how to be in relationships not only with others, but also with myself has been an adventure I never thought possible. Those dreams have become memories, and I am finding that I am losing track of time. Who was I before I transitioned? Who am I now? Who will I be tomorrow? I am pretty sure the answer is: They are all me, but there are so many different versions of me, no wonder I am getting confused.

In my book, *No! Maybe? Yes! Living My Truth*, I am pretty clear that I choose to live in the present moment. I do fully want to and believe that living in the moment is the best way to live one's life. I still dream of possibilities but there are mornings it seems as if they have already happened. Are the memories of my dreams really the dreams of my memories? Have I traveled to another dimension or another timeline when I am in REM sleep—only being pulled back to this place where I exist in this moment?

Last week I met a friend who is early in her exploration and questioning where she might be on her gender journey. I am always glad to be a resource for those who are not as far as I am along their path. There were many girls there for me when I was in my exploration stage. I am happy to answer questions of all types, but clearly pointed out that she needs to talk to many people and figure out her own story and her own answers. It was hard for me to know if my answers were my memories or some dreamlike story that was taking their place. This was my first awareness that I am starting to travel in time. I hope I didn't confuse her too much or set her off on a wrong path. She is comparing her feelings with those she learns from others. I am pretty sure that this is the best way for exploring our gender identity when it does not fit the culturally accepted binary model, so she is doing the right thing.

– ☼ –

I am four years post-transition, and I am again dreaming of possible futures. I hope to make a difference for other people, in ways I do not even know right now. Sometimes I am getting stuck and not living in the present. I think I have some memories of living like this from times long ago. I am thinking hard and deep to find the memories of how I got unstuck and made the choice—some quite hard—to follow my dreams.

Right now, I am stuck in the groove of my memories and dreams and need a little push to jump back to the present. Time traveling does have its benefits. However, I do not want to get stuck there. All I really have is now!

Reflections

Reflections and mirrors are a topic that keeps recurring for me. I ask others and myself "Whose Life Are You Living?" and "Who do you see when you look in a mirror?" I have become OK with asking this every day and not getting stuck with yesterday's answer.

Posted: 04/20/2015

> *See the pretty girl in that mirror there?*
> *Who can that attractive girl be?*
> *Such a pretty face*
> *Such a pretty dress*
> *Such a pretty smile*
> *Such a pretty me!*

– Steven Sondheim, 1957, from *West Side Story*

There have been many days when I did not want to look in a mirror. Many, many days!

Reflections can be funny things. We see reflections of our outer surface, and also have the deep inner reflections that individuals process their way through. How many of the following questions do you reflect on?

o   Who am I?

o   Where do I belong?

o   What am I doing with my life?

o   Will anyone ever really love me?

It is excruciatingly difficult when one is so busy working on an-swering these internal questions and then sees the outer surface reflec-tion does not match the internal one.

I know what this is like! Denying and hiding my struggle with gender identity for close to 60 years has made me familiar with how often the reflection I saw in a mirror belied my true self. Many times it was easier to believe what I saw in my reflection rather than the truth inside of me. After all, isn't what I saw in the mirror the same as how other people saw me? How could I ever hold onto all of those relation-ships if I told them they were not seeing the true me? My inner reflec-tions told me that there would be no possible way. Absolutely no way!

– ☼ –

I was ten years old when *West Side Story* opened on Broadway, and it was not long before I heard the song *"I Feel Pretty"* on the radio. *"See the pretty girl in the mirror there"* was already triggering my internal re-flection. Ten years old and I could not even begin to understand what this meant, and I dare not tell anyone. I was already trying on my mom's clothes when she was not home. I had no idea why, and I could not stop. I climbed on the bed to look in the mirror over the dresser and would dream, and hum that song to myself, while carefully listen-ing to make sure there was not a key scratching to open the front door. I wanted so much to be the girl I saw in the mirror. That girl was defi-nitely inside of me. I knew she was, but there was no way she could get out and be seen except when I would dress up. I also thought that there must be something seriously wrong with me. Life was clearly going to be a challenge.

It took me a long time to realize that I was not alone, and that be-ing transgender is not the only reason that people may struggle with mirrors and reflections. The questions I asked above seem to part of the package of being human. In my almost seven decades working through my life, I have met very few people who do not ask themselves at least one of those questions, either at some point during their life or constantly throughtout it. Perhaps dealing with one's gender identity is not so different than each person's search for his or her own truth. I believe that this is an absolute truth! It is one that we hardly talk about, as we try so hard to fit into some mold that our culture and family teaches us. How many people feel they must, must deny or hide who they truly are?

For those of us who are transgender and choose to be visible in the wider world, perhaps we are becoming a model for others that it is OK to be and express your truth, no matter what it is—of course, within the bounds of doing no harm. Now wouldn't that be something? I have learned that there is nothing wrong with me for being, accepting, and living my truth. I hope that everyone can learn to both *live* their own truth and *accept* others who choose to live and express theirs. I dream of the day when the term "people like us" takes on the meaning of people who are free to be just who they are without any conditions or judgments or discrimination. I like this dream. I like it a lot.

I no longer have my old problem with mirrors. For me it took a long time, and the decision to make my outside match my inside. This is certainly one of many possible solutions available, and each of us needs to find our own.

I have learned to be OK with what I now see in my reflections. My internal picture of who I am is now in alignment with the reflection of my outer self. In the afterword of my book *No! Maybe? Yes! Living my Truth*, I share how valuable reflections are to me now:

She loves watching the snow now. She takes in a very deep breath and calmly squeezes her eyes into a smile that can focus sharply. She closely watches flake after flake float by and is always so curious to see how each is unique.

She doesn't know how, still loving the mystery of it all, but she knows she is connected in some way to each and every snowflake. She loves the warm feeling that flows when she recognizes the beauty in each one of them.

She steps away from the window and catches her own reflection. Her smile steadily grows as she notices the same warm feeling flowing through her entire body as she recognizes the beauty in herself.

Sharing Secrets and Releasing the Shame

This article was a bit of an anniversary article for me. It was posted four years from the date I considered to be my transition date; that of my facial surgery. There was no going back for me. I had no idea what my future would look like or how I would explain so much to so many. The perspective of four years has put it in a different place as I have moved from shame to pride. I will always tell people each person's journey is unique to them. However, it is important to hear many stories and then write your own.

Posted: 04/28/2015

The secret was tearing me apart. I hid for so, so long. Not only from others, but also from myself. I could not even admit it to myself. I became an expert in hiding, denying, and making excuses. I learned that this is a very common experience for people like me, who are transgender.

My inner experience was an inner war that I describe in the introduction of my book, *No! Maybe? Yes! Living My Truth*:

A part of me kept screaming, "Be a Man!"

While another part could not stop laughing while thinking, "Who are you fooling?"

I had a part that got so turned on by girls; that part wanted the sex, the pleasure, the release, the intimacy.

Another part took me to flights of fantasy and then scolded me for hiding my truth.

There were many more... arguing and fighting and judging and criticizing and making all sorts of noise.

These conflicting parts were tearing me apart from different directions. At the time, I had no idea that each had their own single mission—to protect and save me—to save me from something they each thought I could never handle. I tried to shut them all down in many various ways. This proved impossible.

For those of us who come to understand and accept that *we must* transition gender to find inner peace, we know that we are faced with finally telling our secret. It's hard to describe to those who do not experience it. We can watch how others perform their own coming out, but each of us will have to find our own path. There is no other way.

For me, the physical changes were already happening. I was the old guy with the ponytail growing. The day I came into work with my ears pierced everyone made some comment. That only lasted a single day and was attributed to my midlife crisis. I laughed with them on the outside, but was a nervous wreck on the inside. Even so, I knew I had put another checkmark on the transition checklist. I started taking hormones and my body was changing. The tight t-shirts were eliminated from my work clothes and replaced by baggy shirts and sweaters. I purposefully went for electrolysis on Friday evenings, so my face would heal before going back to work on Monday mornings. I managed like this for almost two years.

I had a date for my facial surgery: April 28, 2011. I knew I would be out of work for four weeks healing, so I had to start sharing my secret. It was time. I had a plan and a timeline. I always recommend this to anyone transitioning. First, I told the diversity team and human resources, then senior management, followed by confiding my secret to about a dozen peer level managers. The first time was excruciatingly difficult, but it got easier with each person. When I left work to have my surgery, I didn't tell all the coworkers what was going on. That task was handled the week before I returned with an HR training class held for around two hundred people. I was told it went well. Looking back now, I can certainly say my experience returning to work was positive and amazing. I was fortunate to have the help I got at work.

— ☼ —

We now have seen "The Interview" with Bruce Jenner. I can't help but reflect on how similar his journey seems to be to the one I traveled only a few short years ago. However, there is one big difference.

When I started to share my secret, every single person was surprised. No one had guessed or expected me to announce I would be transitioning my gender. Some got it and some did not, but they all professed support. This was a giant relief and helped relieve my internal shame.

I am sure that the screening of the interview was a huge relief for Jenner. I know because I, too, have walked in those shoes. The path is not easy, internally or externally, but it is a journey that so many need to travel.

— ☼ —

After I transitioned, I started to run workplace trainings like the ones that were done at my company when I transitioned. Over the past few years, I have had the opportunity to train hundreds of people to help them understand what the transition journey is like. When we see someone transition, it is often after many years of hiding and struggling to find self-acceptance. There are stages most people go through to transition. In 2004, Aaron H. Devor, defined these stages in his paper, "Witnessing and Mirroring: A Fourteen-Stage Model of Transsexual Identity Formation." I've shared an info graphic I've developed for my teaching that shows these stages and the transition timeline. It's clear to see many of us hide internally before we accept our truth—long before the actual transition event.

It's critical to note that the transition event is far from the end of the journey for any of us. Perhaps if Jenner does indeed announce his transgender journey, this will give us a better sense of his timeline and the path he has traveled. I suspect that like me and many of us who have found the courage to share our secret, Jenner will reveal he has been on his journey for far longer than anyone may know. Perhaps no one will be surprised given the exhaustive public scrutiny that began when he grew his ponytail and pierced his ears.

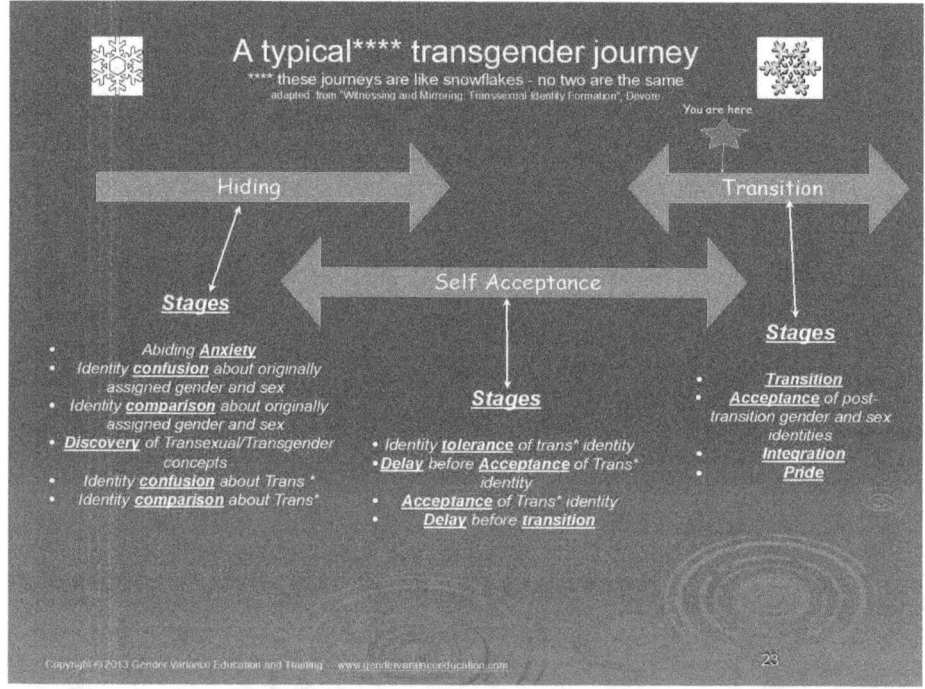

Stages and timeline for transition.

This Old "House"

Dictionary.com defines "allegory" as a representation of an abstract or spiritual meaning through concrete or material forms; figurative treatment of one subject under the guise of another or a symbolical narrative.

When I started writing this post, as usual, I was not quite sure where it was headed. When it was done, I was happily surprised that I wrote an allegory.

Posted: 04/30/2015

It was one of those now classic homes built back in the late forties. It seems so long ago, and in such a different world.

I'm sure you know the kind that I am talking about. So many people after World War II started to build. It was kind of a boom, they say.

Many years later I heard some stories about this one particular home, the one that I lived in.

There were the plans. Construction got underway a few times, but never really took hold. At least once, the foundation was poured but proved too weak, and collapsed. The builders sought help, and they learned that there was an additive that was believed could help strengthen the foundation. Something called DES, so they thought they would try it. Sure enough, it appeared to do the job. A very strong foundation was built, and in August 1947, it was time to move in.

Over the years, this house proved to be durable and able to withstand the forces of the environment—those over time that are expected, and also those of the occasional unexpected storms that happened to all homes. Many times over the decades, we had occasions to redecorate and keep everything new, updated, and in good working condition. These times of renewal always were filled with joy as fresh starts.

For most of these years, much hard work ensured our home matched the other houses in the neighborhood. I was concerned that there would be many problems with the neighborhood if for some reason this house suddenly began to stand out. It took a great deal of energy to make sure this would not happen.

– ☼ –

After 60 years or so, there did not seem to be either enough reason or caring if this house no longer appeared the same as all the other houses in the neighborhood. Being different is not that bad a thing. After all, over those years it seemed that everyone was different in one way or another. Maybe each of these differences is what makes us so special. No more ticky-tacky for this house, no way!

No one knew how different this home was inside compared to what it looked like on the outside. For most of the 60 years, very few people were ever allowed inside to see what was there. It was pretty scary to think about letting anyone even peek inside.

It was time to repeat what the original builders did those many years ago...

I had the plans. Construction got underway a few times, but never really took hold. I sought help and found that my plans were a bit disorganized and not fully formed. I had to take a big step back and figure out how much work it would be and how long it would take, as there was no way it could happen all at once. I also had to plan what I would say if my neighbors asked what was going on, especially if they thought it would negatively impact the neighborhood. Luckily, I never had to deal with that.

With the final plans firmed up, I knew that all the construction work would take a few years, but that was OK with me. A fair amount of preparation work was necessary before any major work was done. Scraping and priming and preparing the old surfaces made them ready for the new coats of paint, which also required being careful with the different chemicals used in this work. It was important to follow the usage directions to assure the desired outcome. In hindsight, I am glad that I did.

Once the prep work was done, the first year required putting a brand new face on the exterior, taking down all the worn clapboard siding and replacing them with new ones. This was a major job and was quite expensive. I knew the roof needed replacement but that was going to be one of the last repairs.

The second year of the plan was to replace the plumbing. The 60-year-old original plumbing still worked fine, but this was more of an aesthetic issue in that it didn't match the new exterior. It took me a while to decide on the right fixtures that I wanted, as only the best would do. Once this was completed, it did take me a while to get used to it all. It was quite different from the original. It took some time, but I have learned to love all the new equipment.

Over the third year I finally got around to the roof. I replace the roof in stages, as I was a bit surprised at the how much the cost of all the renovations was adding up to.

It has been a few years since I completed all the work on this old "house." None of the neighbors ever complained. In fact they seem even friendlier, or perhaps that is actually me who is being friendlier. It is so much easier to chat with them and anyone now, than it used to be. Some even say it has improved the neighborhood. What a pleasant surprise this turned out to be.

I am also taking good care of my house now, and never let it get in to any form of disrepair. I am not sure how much longer I will get to live in this place, but it is finally the home I always dreamed I would have. It really is my home, sweet, home.

Modern Pen Pals

As I became "friends" with more and more people on social media, and Facebook in particular, I became fascinated and confused by what the meaning of these connections really were. Were these connections one, two, three, or of even more dimensions? Were there common journeys, common experiences, or who knows what?

It is almost a year since I wrote Modern Pen Pals.

This past February I was lucky enough to have a training gig in Seattle and had an opportunity to meet not only Jenny but two other modern pen pals, (i.e., Facebook friends).

I had never expected to have such wonderful times in such a random, no, make that synchronous manner. Sharing real meals and real hugs were amazing!

Jenny and I shared a dinner that lasted five hours and were kindly asked to leave the restaurant as they were mostly done cleaning up. Our joint musings could have gone on forever. Yes, the adventure continues, and I am loving the journey.

Posted: 05/07/2015

You might say I am not one of those early adopters. You must know those people; the ones that camp out in front of the local Apple store days before the next iGadget comes out. No, I never have been and probably never will be.

Grace and Jenny finally met in person, February 2016.

There are some ideas it has taken me decades to catch on to. Having a pen pal is one of them. I remember way back in the fifties I had classmates who talked about writing to their pen pals. They told me their pen pals were in countries that at the time I had never even heard of, let alone knew where they were. Back then most people who went on an overseas vacation traveled by ocean liner. The world was very different.

As you probably know by now, even way back then, there were parts of me in hiding, and I could not even imagine writing about personal feelings to another person. I never was able to articulate what exactly was going on, but I knew that when I secretly would dress in my mom's clothes, that was not what all the other boys were doing. No! I never had a pen pal.

Until now!

I was a late adopter to social media. I did not get involved until after I transitioned my gender in 2011 and no longer felt the need to hide. I am not sure when the word "friend" became a verb, as used on Facebook. "Friend me" has seemed to replace "see you later" when you meet someone new. I hardly ever used the later, but I have learned to say, "Friend me."

Many, but not all of my Facebook friends are transgender. There is a large and most interestingly diverse community that has at least one thing in common: They have at the very least, questioned or been confused that their gender assigned at birth does not consistently align with their psychological sense of who they are or how they want to express themselves. I am not sure if I have a lot of Facebook friends compared to other people, but it sure seems like it is so for me.

I have conversations, both public and private with many people whom I suspect I will never meet. Welcome to the modern world! Sometimes there are multiple Facebook chats going on at the same time. When this occurs it can be confusing as to what I am saying to whom. Although these are friends, I suspect that I will never meet most of them. I guess this is my modern version of having pen pals.

However, a few people are both "friends" and friends. I am still not sure if I will ever meet them, but there does appear to more of that feeling…that feeling of *simpatico*…sort of kindred spirits that somehow enhance a conversation, a friendship, even if it is distant and just written in the new virtual world. I think this is what my classmates were talking about over 50 years ago. That was how they described their pen pals. Yes, I am a late adopter, but as with so many other events in my life, I have learned it is never too late for anything. Now I have a pen pal.

Jenny lives on the West Coast, and I am not quite sure how we connected. Sometimes I adore the mysterious way the universe works. We are in the same age group and both active in our local transgender communities. We both can seamlessly jump our conversations between the serious, the sublime, and the various escapist worlds we both spend some time in. We reference old shows and musicals and have fun testing each other on our knowledge of 1950s TV shows. This has often gone on and on. Jenny is my pen pal in that old 1950s trivial sense too. We are not sure if we will ever meet, but we agree that if we do, we will probably be talking nonstop for a number of days until we both drop from exhaustion.

I got an email from Jenny, in which she apologized for what she thought was an offense to me (it wasn't), which was so beautiful. It inspired me to think about the fact that once I stopped hiding, I learned to have friends in many places.

Jenny wrote the following:

And then a gentle Spring breeze came and blew through the bamboo garden of my mind last night, freeing it from all of the accumulated dead undergrowth. The feeling of lightness and peace after climbing back is tangible! To awaken this morning to the sun, to absorb it, to feel it, to know once again that sense of life coursing through me.

When I chose to live my life as my true self, I did, as Jenny has suggested, "freeing my mind from all the accumulated undergrowth." This made space for me to find friends, and be a friend. Living your truth may well be a spring breeze.

This may be a good time for a Spring-cleaning. Not just for me, perhaps for you too. It is never too late!

Whose Life Are You Living?

I have been a fan of Joseph Campbell since I had watched all of the Bill Moyers PBS programs on The Power of Myth. *I acquired all of the videos I could about Campbell and I even gave copies of The Joseph Campbell Reader to my adult sons, as something I hoped they may find useful as a guidebook for their lives. I know there was a part of me, doing this to try to make up for some of my (own perceived) failures as a father. Today I speak on the very question above and hope to encourage and inspire everyone to find and live his or her truth.*

Posted: 05/14/2015

> *You enter the forest*
> *at the darkest point,*
> *where there is no path.*
> *Where there is a way or path,*
> *it is someone else's path.*
> *You are not on your own path.*
> *If you follow someone else's way,*
> *you are not going to realize*
> *your potential.*

– Joseph Campbell

It took a long time before I found my own path.

In all truth, I had no idea that the possibility of having my very own path existed. Sure, I struggled internally for as long as I can remember. However, no one was ever aware of this struggle. It makes me feel good that no one knowing may have been true, but I did live in one form of isolation or another for so many years. There were layers and layers of masks in all of my relationships. That's just the way it was, and I had no idea it could ever be anything different.

I followed the baby boomer American Dream path. Go to college; get a degree; get a good job; get married; have kids; buy a house, and ultimately a small fleet of cars; coach the kids sports; send them off to college, and then...get divorced. Find an apartment; start new relationships, and then...

And then...come home from work each night and cry, and cry, and cry.

As the flood of tears slowed down, I asked myself: "Whose life am I living?" That question was a hard one, but not nearly as hard as trying to answer it—followed by more crying and adding some new masks to the old ones with the unanswered question slowly melting in the puddle of tears.

No path existed for me to follow for some time as I was aimlessly wandering through my life. Perhaps this was my own version of 40 years in the desert wilderness surviving on the manna of a single new relationship and searching for a spiritual center, all while knowing the remnants of unanswered questiona were hidden away deep inside me. Who am I? Whose life am I living? Every now and again, they pushed through the pile of masks and then the tears again followed quickly.

This time, it was different. As I looked back, it seemed so much of my life was behind me. I recalled so many wonderful events and memories.

Yet, that gnawing question started with a different tack. Did I recognize that person who was wearing all of the masks in all those wonderful scenes? Did I? Did I? The voice kept pestering me, and now would not stop.

Author pre-transition.

I no longer experienced the endless flow of tears, but now a tangible pain ran from the back of my head down my back and tightened my diaphragm. The "yes" that automatically was verbalized slowly became a "no" as I finally began to see how long I was hiding—hiding from myself—hiding from my truth. Could I, would I, be willing to see this truth, search for this truth, even accept this truth? Many questions were being asked that I couldn't answer at that time. The tightness in my stomach grew and grew.

But this was a path I knew I must follow. It was no one else's path, but mine alone. I was afraid; very, very afraid. I am pretty sure a part of me had an idea where it would lead and had worked quite hard to prevent me from going there.

Our fears are like dragons guarding our most precious treasures.

– Rilke

I knew I had to move forward and answer each one of these long unanswered questions.

This new path tested me in ways I never dared face before. I had to throw out mask after mask and be willing to be seen. Not only by others, but by myself as well. That tightness in my stomach continued for most of this journey without letup, and yet, I chose to keep moving forward.

I was being pushed from inside, and it also felt that something outside of me was pulling me forward. I still do not fully understand this force, but can now express gratitude that it was present. This could not have just been all me, right?

I answered the question and found that I was not living my true life. This path was not easy to travel. There were monsters and demons that had to be faced, many of my own making, and only I could tame and learn to live with and love. Only then was I able to move forward to live my true life.

I thought that the path would end then, but I was so very wrong. Once I chose to live true to myself, I found so many new pathways branching off in all directions, each with welcoming new adventures and challenges of their own. The pain in my neck, diaphragm, and stomach are long gone. Even when I look back at all those memories, I can recognize the old versions of myself and can feel so much compassion to each of them.

If you struggle with the question, "Whose life are you living?" I suggest you first grab some tissues and see if you can find a path that is not someone else's. I do not know where it will lead nor do you. You're the only one that can take it. It may be the only way for you to answer the question.

Commencement Dreams

Time traveling and dreams are a pretty consistent and inspirational source of my writings. I like the definition of dreams as a form of practicing for some future event. I am glad that I am still a dreamer, even if some are in the middle of the day!

Posted: 05/21/2015

I have always been a dreamer.

When I was young, perhaps it was the method I used to escape from each present moment where I knew I did not fully fit.

However, even today when I have been on such an incredible journey where so many of my dreams have come true, I am still a dreamer.

The other day I had a dream, which I suspect was inspired by watching all the news reports about graduations and the various graduation speakers. After all, it is the middle of May and each day provides a new report of some politician or celebrity sharing their wisdom of life with freshly minted graduates. This dream had me draped in the obligatory robes, and walking up on stage and giving a commencement speech. Some people say that dreams are the way we practice for some future event, and to be honest, this has been an item on my own bucket list. But, that is just one of my conscious dreams.

I know that although dreams seem to take a long, long time, the actual dreaming event occurs in a relatively short time. Our REM sleep, in addition to paralyzing our body, provides us a sense of time and space that takes us to many places. The speech I gave was short, and inspired by what I believe was the experience and learning of my life. After all, isn't that what the wisdom of these speeches is all about? It was about the future of every moment. I paraphrased the title from something that Bill Belichick said after the Patriots' fourth game this past year when things looked darkest for the team, and he refused to talk about the past. Here is my Bill Belichick speech.

"On To Tomorrow"

I once had a boss whom I thought was pretty arrogant. It ticked me off when he said, "I thought I made a mistake once, but I was wrong!" I was having my own internal battle of wanting to be right all the time, but there were so many examples in my life that the facts did not support. Oh, so many examples. When I made a mistake, I found it hard to learn from it and move on. I often dwelled in it for what seemed to be immeasurable moments and could not concentrate on anything else. There was a critical part of me that would not stop berating myself, and used so many epithets I don't ever want to hear again—either from inside of me or out! It was hard to smile or converse with any other people, as the self-inflicted punishment seemed endless. In fact, it was! Even when my inner voices quieted down, I knew the inner critic was still there, stored deep down and was eager to appear at the next mistake I made and start all over again.

It took me decades to understand why I always wanted to be right. I knew, that deep inside of me I was different from everyone else, and that if anyone found out how different I was, they would want nothing to do with me. I had many parts that feared that potential loss more than anything. The strongest of these voices thought that if I was always right, people would look up to me, listen to me, and I would be involved and part of their lives. I would never have to reveal the real me, and everything would be fine. It had no idea that this never quite worked the way I planned.

There came the day that I spoke up to those internal voices that were beating me up and told them that nothing seemed to be working.

I was stuck in not being me, and all the hiding and protecting still did not bring me close to anyone, and all my dreams that were piling up in the corner of my mind started to stink from an internal rot. I was tired of hiding and protecting and being berated.

I wanted tomorrow to be different. I no longer wanted to live in the past. I no longer needed to be right all the time. I would be OK with making a mistake and be willing to learn from it and move on to be who I really am. I would be OK with being different than others because after all, this is the real me—the only me I have.

I learned from my mistakes. I really did. I learned to not dwell in the past, or beat myself up. I learned to learn from every experience I have, and look forward to the next adventure. Most of all, I have learned to move "on to tomorrow!"

Truth be told, this is the speech that I tell my own internal audience to commence every day. It has taken most of my 60-something years to reach the point where my parts and voices are willing to listen and are comfortable with the message, and trust that we can all together handle the adventures that appear for us each day. We have learned to trust each other on this adventure and look forward to the amazement of each tomorrow.

Every morning I still wake up with the remnants of a fresh dream floating from my mind. Some days it is a battle to hold onto them before they dissolve right in front of me. Some days, they stick like glue, and I cannot let them go.

Yes, I have always been a dreamer. I hope this never stops.

Walking in His/Her Shoes

Well, it is a bit like the elephant in the room. The Jenner Journey in the public eye was now underway. When I wrote this, it was post announcement but as yet, pre-transition. My expectations were as great as most in the trans community. I struggled as I used my small platform for political statements, and I fought with my publicist on feeding and creating conflict. I was hoping to express my thoughts and opinions in a consumable and yet hopeful manner. I am still not sure if I was successful.

Posted: 05/28/2015

I have experienced so many transitions.

There were the decades of saying "no," to just about everything in my path as I was filled with fears I could not or would not dare name. At the age of 54, and the end of my 25-year marriage, with my children all now budding adults, I was alone and had to accept that my lifetime of saying "no," had not led me to a sustainable place. Perhaps change was not so bad, not so evil. Perhaps I could change if I was truly willing to face some of my fears.

In my book, *No! Maybe? Yes! Living My Truth*, I share my journey of coming to accept my gender identity and gender transition. However, there is so much more about many other transitions in my life that are also important.

Even compared to my gender transition, which required finding the strength to align my inner world, which was always present and hidden, with my outer world, I still find my transition from a Type-A engineering manager to that of a counselor/therapist a more challenging journey.

From being the person who thought he knew every answer for every problem (for every person) to becoming the woman I am now, who can sit with someone, hold a safe space, listen, and find her center of empathy to feel what she is feeling, is a journey that I believe few actually take. Interestingly, I can look at the world and the people I meet through both sets of eyes, as I really try to feel what others are feeling. Instead of telling them what to do, I ask how I can best support them.

— ☼ —

It was with both these sets of eyes, that I have been watching the "About Bruce" episodes on the Kardashian shows. Even with the pretty uniform positive media and online comments after the Diane Sawyer interview, most of the chatter that I have seen within the trans community about expectations of this further exposure was negative and less than open. I, myself, was not certain what to expect or if I even wanted to watch any of it. It would be the first time I would be watching any of these Kardashian shows. My first-hand knowledge of all of them was slim, if any.

As I watched it, I was fascinated, triggered, amazed, and confused, but most of all, I found that by the end of each segment, I was finding a deep sense of empathy arise within me for each person and his or her experience.

As a leader within New England's transgender community, I always advise each new person to listen to everyone's story and then find his or her own. Each person's story, their life, their experience, is unique. I know and advise that there is no one single or right way to take your journey. I also needed to listen to my own advice as I watched the Jenner family's story unfold. I am glad that I did.

— ☼ —

My engineer's eyes were analyzing what I saw, but not really listening to the content. I was looking at the big picture, getting the full map of the territory, listing all the players, and checking if they had an agenda. While doing this, the engineer was also jotting down comments and judgments on each one of these topics that could be of use later. Over 40 years of experience made this practice easy.

My counselor's eyes were not analyzing at all. They were concentrating on the words and watching the emotions and body language, and steering them to my own inner places to see if I could understand and relate to what they saw and what I was hearing. Moment after moment, I heard the words that not only I have spoken in the past but I have heard from so many other people I know in the trans community. What I saw was drawing so much empathy from deep inside me. I have walked in these shoes.

Many people ask why someone would transition gender in their sixties. I have walked in these shoes.

Yes, responsibility to family often overrides the inner battle.

Bruce hid his truth from his wife. I have walked in these shoes.
Reality is hiding the truth from oneself until it cannot stay hidden.

Kim told Bruce, "No neon!" I have walked in these shoes.
Wanting to be seen but not really showing what is inside.

Each of the kids has responded with a different set of feelings and level of understanding. I have walked in these shoes.
The kids are all unique too, and the best part is that they talk to each other. This is so much better than being abandoned.

– ☼ –

I am pretty sure that these shows will never be on my regular must-see list, but I was able to separate the larger-than-life reality show, the reported money-making machine, and found I could identify with the human feelings that the family expressed, as I am very familiar with the content of what was said, and have lived with myself, and know many others who have also lived it.

Jenner stated that he will change the world. Perhaps he will, perhaps he has already.

Through my own transitions, I have learned what a challenging task it is to change the world. I have learned that the best I can do is perhaps make a difference to one person at a time. There is a saying that comes from the Talmud:

Whoever saves a life, it is considered as if he has saved the world.

I have learned the first step in making a difference is to listen, to hear, to walk in his or her shoes, with love and acceptance. Empathy.

Cover Girls and Tipping Points

Week 2 of the Jenner Journey! The rumors were flying about a Vanity Fair *cover. I still wanted to hold out hope, but was worried what this was going to be like.*

Posted: 06/01/2015

What a difference a year makes!

As a transgender woman dedicated to teaching acceptance and living our own truth, I want to ask every person I meet to pinch me, to make sure I am awake and not dreaming all of what has happened. Pinch me, please... thanks, I am awake, yes, but I am still a bit numb taking this all in.

It was only last June, that Laverne Cox was the cover girl of *TIME Magazine*, which proclaimed, "The Transgender Tipping Point," and discussed this as America's next civil rights frontier. For many people both within and outside the transgender community, it seemed like a tree truly did tip over, and when it hit the ground, so many of us could feel the earth move.

Over the past year, we have seen many models not only come out as transgender, but also transition in the public eye. *The New York Times* in its "Transgender Today" series is now publishing the stories of as many transgender people who choose to contribute. There hardly seems to be a day going by where there is not another story or blog about one or another aspect of being gender variant (not fitting into a strict binary, male or female construct). I know I am contributing right here.

JUNE 9, 2014

TI**N**E

THE TRANSGENDER TIPPING POINT

America's next
civil rights frontier
BY KATY STEINMETZ

Laverne Cox, a star
of *Orange Is the New
Black*, is one of an
estimated 1.5 million
Americans who identify
as transgender

time.com

Laverne Cox on the cover of *TIME Magazine*.

Yet, with all this exposure, all this visibility, that in my mind is all good and making such a huge difference in understanding and acceptance, I know I was thinking there could not be another major magazine cover girl that could get the attention of the public in a way that occurred with Laverne Cox last June.

But now I wonder if this is true. Perhaps as Yoda told Obi Wan, (when Luke left to help Han and Leia before his Jedi training was completed) "There is another!"

We now hear reports that the July issue of *Vanity Fair* will be of Ms. (*her*) Jenner. This will be our first time meeting her, and perhaps by then, we will learn her proper name. Reports tell us that Annie Leibovitz will or has done this photo shoot, so at the very least, it is certain to be striking. However, we do know that *Vanity Fair* is no stranger to controversy, so I am wondering what the captions for this cover might proclaim as the editors decide what they are going to communicate.

— ☼ —

Tipping points are funny things. I learned this the hard way. Both as a Boy Scout, with a small and then larger axe learning to chop down some small trees, to in later years as a homeowner, with that great and scary toy of a gas powered chain saw. I never quite learned to get the trees to fall exactly where I wanted. No matter how clever I thought I was, no matter how much I calculated the angles, it seemed I lacked the skill to know exactly where they would drop. The impact on the surroundings was often hard to deal with. I learned to use a wedge, but I came to know that getting trees to tip where I wanted was a learned skill and took a great deal of practice. So often the learning examples were not pain free.

It took me a long time to accept that when I try something new, even after I read about it and learn everything I can, the only true learning is by doing and accepting the mistakes and errors that the experiences will teach. Reading Malcolm Gladwell's books *The Tipping Point* and *Outliers* has helped me to understand the phenomenon of needing ten thousand hours of practice to become an expert. It is OK to make mistakes as long as we can learn from them. This idea truly came in handy for me during the early days of my own gender transition, and for anyone who will listen, I will advise always taking baby steps and making sure you are on solid ground.

— ☼ —

There is the famous thought experiment: If a tree falls in a forest, and no one is around to hear it, does it make a sound?

We know that one year ago, the sound of the *TIME Magazine* cover was heard very loudly around the world. The last circulation numbers I found (from 2013) showed the magazine at over three million copies. At that time, *Vanity Fair* circulation was reported about a third of that at just over one million copies in circulation. It should be interesting to listen to the sound—I am sure there will be one—when Ms. Jenner becomes a cover girl.

I don't know if all the angles have been calculated and the wedges put in the proper place to make certain that the tipped tree lands exactly where they want it. I sure hope so, as there are so many beautiful surroundings that we need to keep whole. Tipping points are tricky things, and I sure hope we keep these trees tipping in the right direction.

I Feel the Earth Move

Week 3 of the Jenner Journey. It has happened: The yin and the yang of the word "transgender" hitting the world's population smack between the eyes. There were the ayes and the nays. There was no mistake that the earth moved and the territory was about to change. My inner geek took over and tried to give an analogy of a way to look at it both close up and perhaps from a distance of time. I was worried as to what might happen. It is still downright confusing to me as the yin and yang continue the challenge of finding their balance.

Posted: 06/05/2015

> *I feel the earth move under my feet*
> *I feel the sky tumbling down*
> *I feel my heart start to trembling*
> *Whenever you're around*

– Carole King, "I Feel the Earth Move"

There is an old adage: "The map is not the territory." It seems to me, that one needs to gain the wisdom of experience to understand the meaning of this. The release of the *Vanity Fair* cover story "Call Me Caitlyn" *made my heart start to trembling* and *I felt the earth move under my feet.*

It was Monday, June 1, 2015, that the landscape changed forever as if the entire planet was slammed by Thor's hammer, *Mjolnir*, as we were introduced to Caitlyn Jenner in all her cover girl beauty and glory. Vast amounts of support have been reported far and wide on Jenner's courage on now beginning to express and live as her authentic self.

Once again we hear that an event has broken the Internet. I myself have been quoted in multiple places that this event is so important in that the transgender community could not pay for this amount of visibility. The word "transgender" is now on the lips of millions, and many have uttered it for the first time. Some know what it means, some are curious, and still some either casually or vehemently dismiss and disparage it. The discussion of gender and gender variance is no longer in the dark, on the sly, or something to avoid. Understanding and accepting what it all is, implies, and means is, as they say, another story. However, make no mistake, the earth has moved, the world has changed, the Internet was broken. When these types of events occur, the territory has changed too, and the old maps no longer give you the correct directions.

When an earthquake occurs, it takes many, many people to clean up and figure out what was broken and have the energy and the wherewithal to learn how to traverse the new territory and create the new maps. We have learned to send in our best and most experienced people to support these events whether they are physical or figurative. At least I hope we have.

Caitlyn Jenner and perhaps Team Caitlyn wielded the hammer this week that changed the world, and at least for a moment, or a day, I suspect she felt she was on the top of world. For Caitlyn this may not have been an unfamiliar feeling.

For those who are familiar with some of my writings here, you know I like to share stories about some of my old bosses. Here is another. One of my former bosses used to say, "When you get to the top of the pyramid, there is only room to keep one foot on the point, and it is easy to lose your balance and fall back down the side to the bottom."

As I write this just two days after the earth has moved, and my heart, like many others, started to trembling, we see the first promo for "I Am Cait" and at least for me, it appears that Ms. Jenner may have already lost her balance at the top of the world. Perhaps she truly believes she will change the world, but the simple phrase exclaimed in this trailer where she says "I'm the new normal" has me deeply concerned. It is just a snippet, and I could be missing the overall context, but I think not. Ms. Jenner is neither the first, nor will she be the last person who crosses the gender divide. She is, probably the most visible person. She is but one of many who each follow their own unique path to living their authentic life. This is a goal of many but far from the new normal.

I think that I can speak to this with a sense of experience, as I, myself, have transitioned gender at the age of 64 and am now over four years down this road. I cannot even imagine anyone, let me repeat this, *anyone*, early on their transition journey claiming to be the new normal, or even suggesting they represent anyone but him- or herself. I have many friends in all age groups that have been on similar journeys and not a single one has made a claim like this. For me and many of those I know, this was a time of self-discovery and self-reflection, and for many a chance to make up for a different time of puberty they may have missed. However, each and every one of us knew that this was our individual journey and not a model for anyone else.

Clearly this promo has triggered me. As a transgender woman, as a therapist, as a teacher on gender variance, I am concerned where this docuseries will be going and whether this will help to clean up and create the new and correct maps for the new territory.

I worry if Caitlin has lost her balance. She has had the ability to wield the hammer that has changed the world. We know that if the hammer was Mjolnir, it is engraved as follows:

"Whosoever holds this hammer, if s/he be worthy, shall possess the power of Thor."

I believed that at least for a few days that Caitlyn appeared to be worthy of wielding the hammer. I am now not sure that this is true.

I believe that the cleanup work should be left to the experts. Those of us who have been doing this work for years and have the wisdom to know what we are talking about, and the experience of having been through this journey already. In time Caitlyn will learn to truly know herself and find her true voice, I have no doubt. I applaud her for changing the landscape. She has done what only she was able to do. I hope she can recognize this and be able to recognize what she is good at, and make room for those who can continue to accomplish the goals she desires.

Teaching Moments: Where Is Caitlyn?

Week 4 of the Jenner Journey—and for me the end of this thread focusing on it. I attempted to go back to becoming a teacher rather than a critic. This helped me reduce my own anger and allowed me to ask myself once again whose life am I living? What is my message and what is my mission? I believe I walked away from the past month with a new clarity as to my own path and how to stay focused on writing what was important to me, no matter where it might take me. It felt so much better to get to this place on my own journey.

Posted: 06/10/2015

Having hid for so many decades, from both myself and all those in my life, at first the idea of being seen—yes really being seen by everyone—seemed to take over. When I transitioned in 2011, my day job in the tech world was on a campus of over a thousand people, and my role did not allow me to be invisible. My evening job as a mental health counselor in a substance abuse clinic was also a place far from transparent. Whether I led with the fact I was transgender or needed to respond to comments or question, over time, I learned that each moment could be a teaching moment.

This did not happen day one for me. No, far from it! There were the comments that triggered me, annoyed me, and even had me questioning everything about my journey. This is the point. The beauty of time is that we can learn, we can grow, and most importantly, we can change.

I knew on the day(s) that marked my transition to become Grace, I did not fully know who Grace was. I knew who I wasn't, but this was the start of a new journey of self-discovery, and finding my real voice. I chose this path without having any idea where it would lead. In my book, *No! Maybe? Yes! Living My Truth*, I wrote about my time of transition:

> *I, too, was reaching the edge of a cliff and was preparing to take a leap. However, I did not have a parachute strapped to my back. No matter how much I was preparing to take this leap, I had no equipment, no security, and no idea where I would land.*

In my last blog, I stated that the map is not the territory, and one needs to gain the wisdom of experience to really understand the meaning of this. Having landed on the ground and spending the past four years discovering who Grace is, reinventing and reunifying myself in ways I had never foreseen, I understand the value of this experience more than ever.

As a parent it took me some time to be comfortable with letting my kids have their learning experiences, making their mistakes, and becoming their own person. In some manner, I had to take this learning and apply it to myself as a "loving parent" would to the newborn version of me named Grace. I made my mistakes, learned, changed, and grew. Most importantly, I learned that this never stops.

The World Professional Association for Transgender Health (WPATH) has published Standards of Care (SOC) that many practitioners follow as the best practices in working with and guiding gender variant people. Although not without controversy, this is the best guidance that is available. There is the concept of The Real Life Test, where it is recommended that an individual live in the new gender for a year before a recommendation for any gender confirmation surgery is provided. It is my experience—both my own and from observing many friends and acquaintances, that this year is of great value in providing a time for self-reflection and really getting to know our new selves. I know that my feelings evolved and changed and certainly had their ups and downs.

This brings me to wonder where Caitlyn is on her journey and perhaps how I would advise her. I do have a map—even though it is not the territory. In 2004 Aaron Devor published a paper titled "Witnessing and Mirroring: A Fourteen-Stage Model of Transsexual Identity Formation." I have adapted it below.

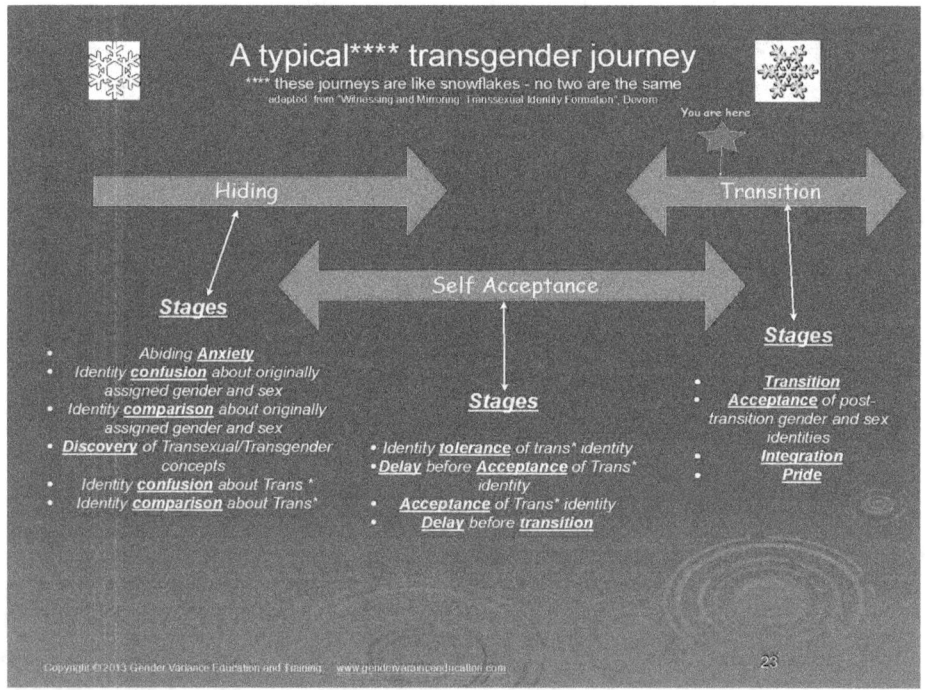

Transgender journey.

The timeline above shows that Caitlyn appears to be very close to the transition event, which is marked by the star. It appears to me, that Caitlyn is at the beginning of the stage: acceptance of post-transition gender and sex identities. As I believe each of our journeys is unique as are snowflakes, there is no specific time duration as we work through the stages. I have had friends that have gone through various experiences and changes. Some of the comments that I have heard include:

"Don't expect me to dress age appropriately"

"Well, that was my slut period"

"Well I never was a teenage girl, so what did you expect?"

The new "hatchling" Caitlyn is going to take us on a road trip as she explores and discovers her voice and who she is. I expect that she will learn a great deal and make great personal discoveries. I know so many people who have done this—including myself. I truly hope that everyone understand this. Caitlyn, like each and every one of us, is a work in progress. Sometime this is hard for us to admit. Caitlyn may fall, she may trip, she may learn, but I am certain she will grow. That will be her journey and hers alone—no one else's.

She appears to be allowing us to watch her go through this. This may be her real courage!

This past February I had the chance to do a corporate training for over six hundred people where a co-worker was transitioning. For scheduling, it was broken into three, one-hour sessions with about two hundred people each time in the room. It was both an intimate and interactive setting. At one session, at Q&A, one person stated, "So, you have spent the past hour asking us just to be a decent human being, right?" I agreed and ended the training there as the teaching moment was complete.

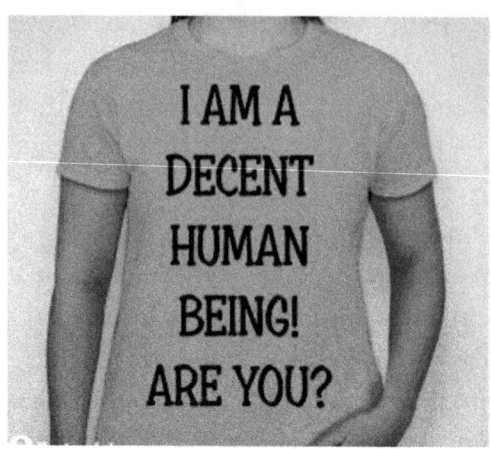

A teaching moment.

Father's Day...and You Thought Pronouns Were Complicated!

When these articles first appeared, my bio described me as the "father of three." I was only a bit surprised when someone commented with the question of how I could be a father? I ignored it as others came to my defense, and I watched the ongoing conversation. Across the transgender community, there are many people with many ways of describing their history and relationships. When I teach, I explain that there is no single way, no one right way to do this. Boxes and labels are hard and no matter how we may want it to be simple, it just doesn't work like that. I do not think we need these labels to be a decent human being. Do you?

Posted: 06/15/2015

I've said it over and over again. I am one of the lucky ones. I've lost no one in my immediate or extended family when I transitioned. I am not going into the whys and wherefores; I am just happy to count my blessings.

There is only a single tradition that I have created since I transitioned, and it is now the time of year that it takes place. I reissue a private blog I ever wrote two years ago. The only thing that has changed is that it is now four years since I transitioned, but I still feel exactly the same:

I'm Still (a) Dad
This Sunday is Father's day.

Now, two years after my transition, I am really thinking about this. Changing genders is such a totally personal decision to throw away the masks, the fear, and the confusion and put oneself out in the world as honestly and authentically as one can. For me, my transition occurred when my three children were already adults and living on their own. I love Jenny Boylan's new memoir Stuck in the Middle with You where her transition occurred when her kids were young, and she also transitioned from father to mother—in name and deed. We know that gender roles are not as rigid perhaps as they used to be, and by being authentic, she points out her boys have become better men.

My kids grew up with a dad who filled all the expected dad roles. I was there teaching and coaching baseball and basketball for many years. I did the driving, the grilling, mowing the lawn, growing the garden, training the dog, helping with the homework—and loved every minute of it. I was also somewhat controlling and thinking that I knew better than everyone, which as I know now was one of my methods of hiding what was inside me.

A few years ago, when I told the kids that I was transgender, my biggest fear was that they would abandon me. Each of them, I believe, has processed my transition in a different manner, but I have not lost any of them. Sometimes we chat about it, and I believe that still having them in my life is another blessing that I have been given.

I am now the woman I knew I was. Each day I awake with gratitude that I am living another day as my authentic self. I have never been the mother of my kids. I have been their father, and that is still part of who I am. Recently I was at a training at the local Apple store and a woman sat next to me who I recognized as the mother of one of my daughter's school friends. She knows my family very well, but I have not seen her in at least 10 years. I said hello and asked her if she knew who I was (I do look different). She was confused and apologized that she did not recognize me, and I explained that I was Stella's dad. It took her a while for that to sink in, but then we were able to chat.

Presently, two of my kids call me Grace, and the other still calls me dad. It must be confusing for them. I am OK with whatever makes them comfortable.

Over the past two years I have changed a great deal. However, there is least one thing that hasn't: I am still (a) dad.

An older version of Author coaching little league in 1987.
Photo by Maxine Bauer, *Lexington Minute Man.*

When one transitions, it is confusing for many of the people in their lives to get the new pronouns correct. When the person who transitions is a parent, it is not only pronouns that will change. Each person and their families have to adjust to the proper use of parental labeling and naming. Like the unique snowflakes we each are, there is no one way, and there are no rules on how to do this. Each person and family has to explore and possibly negotiate this territory in a way that hopefully satisfies everyone. Needless to say, this can be complicated. The transitioning parent may have a strong desire of a new label. Whether or not the children are willing or even allowed to share their thoughts can be an issue.

In my book, *No! Maybe? Yes! Living My Truth*, I had a chance to talk to my son Elie about his experience of meeting Grace.

I think that maybe when we first met Grace...I was thinking that, and it is the same thing now as it was then, when I sit down talking to you...I...don't see Grace really...I just see you...the person who I know. You had all this surgery, and you have all these clothes, and you paint your nails...as my dad...all this, it didn't change to me, you know, your face didn't change drastically enough so I still just recognize you as my dad...so calling you Grace, and sometimes, just stepping away I say, yeah, I guess this is a different person, but to me you don't seem that different in the long run.

I feel like your identity in the world was Father! And you knew how to play that role like in movies and TV—Man—Father. You did sporty things but you did other things, like you sewed and you cooked. But I feel like...You wore sneakers and jeans and a flannel shirt...and a beard at times...and you were a hard person at work. How's your day? Fine! You coached sports; you did the traditional things.

I hope this is not all that offensive, but I feel that Grace is not as feminine as I expected her to be. You wear a ball cap, and your hair is pretty short. You showed me those glam pictures, and I guess that was what I was expecting you to be all the time. And you still wear T-shirts. You switched all your blue jackets to pink jackets, but they are still like Northface ski jackets...and I think that probably in the long run helps because I expected you to be really over the top.

No matter how I saw myself, I am pretty sure that I knew how my kids saw me. I was their dad, and I am still their dad. Even this is complicated as their dad is now a woman named Grace Stevens, and that is often hard for them to explain.

I have never felt I needed to rewrite my history. How I felt internally was as real as how I lived and acted externally in my relationships with family, friends, and co-workers. There were no lies. I never believed that my gender dysphoria could or would justify me to live or act badly to anyone in my life. Yes, it has been complicated!

I am pretty sure the only thing about it that is not complicated is that we are still a family and it is love that holds us together. Happy Father's Day.

Where Do the Children Play?

I was looking forward to this day of adventure and considered my-self blessed to be a "fly on the wall." I was just an observer here, but was blessed to take part in it.

Posted: 06/22/2015

I know we've come a long way
We're changing day to day
But tell me, where do the children play?

– Cat Stevens

It was early Friday morning as I entered my car and held down the home button on my phone. The familiar message appeared, "What can I help you with?" I spoke into it, "Directions to ESPN, Bristol, Connecticut." The day's adventure had begun.

I met Stephen Alexander a little over a month ago, and he graciously invited me to attend a panel discussion he was going to be on at ESPN on transgender athletes. I was a "fly on the wall" as I got to meet some amazing and great people who were sharing their stories with ESPN's internal employee LGBT group, which was also internally broadcast within the parent Disney corporate world. The title of the discussion was "Understanding the T: Transgender Athletes and the Challenge to Compete." ESPN's **Christina Kahrl** was the moderator of this panel, which included:

o **Stephen Alexander**, America's first openly transgender multi-sports coach www.transitiongames.com

o   **Chloie Johnson**, transgender CrossFit athlete

o   **Chris Mosier,** transgender duathlon athlete and a member of Team USA, www.transathlete.com

o   **Wade Davis**, executive director of the You Can Play Project, www.youcanplayproject.org

o   **Jazz Jennings** and her mom on the phone.

It strikes me that we see and hear about someone in the trans community on a daily basis. We hear the good stories, the sad stories, and the outrageous, sensationalized, and indescribable stories. It is easy for many to lose sight that transgender people are first and fore-most people, each trying hopefully to live their best possible life, with-out a burden of being defined by being transgender. I continue to say that we are all so much more than just gender.

Recently, when Janet Mock appeared on Oprah's "Super Soul Sun-day" program, she stated, "For most people the most interesting part of me is my transness." This conversation was about her willingness to own her transness in order to make a positive difference for others in the world. For the athletes above, their discussion points out that their transness, which is their authenticity, has blocked them and so many other trans people from being involved, playing, and competing in sports as who they truly are. Each of their stories and experience is unique. As such, each is an important building block to help all people learn that transgender athletes hold no special advantages and are just people trying to live, work, and play like most of us desire to do.

By being in the audience this was a time for me to have many learning moments as I listened to the participants. Here are some of the comments I heard.

Chloie told the group that she never thought of herself as being transgender. She was just female, period. She said she transitioned at the age of 16 and was never an athlete until she got into competitive CrossFit a few years ago, and was outed by the organization's refusal to allow her to compete, as she was not assigned female at birth. She shared that it was never her intent to be public or an activist but only to stand up for her rights and those of others. Chloie appeared to know this was important, but it was clear that her primary goal was to just live her life. At this point in time, her transness has blocked her from her life's passion.

Chris shared that prior to his transition when he was competing in women's triathlons, he never felt he belonged, as he did not feel like a woman. His personal challenge was to believe he could compete, his passion, if and when he transitioned. Not only was he able to compete, but he has now become a member of Team USA. However, there are still many rules that may hold him back from competing at the highest levels of his sport. He reported that he has achieved one goal, making the team, but there are still many blocks in his path to compete as he desires. He told us it is not the winning that matters; it is the chance to perform that is important. I was able to relate to this from my experience as a coach of little league sports for many years.

Stephen has proved to be perhaps the prodigal son, and shown that one can go home again. Prior to his transition, Stephen had guided his high school girls teams to multiple state championships, and now post-transition he has returned to that very same school and coaches five different sports. Stephen is putting himself on the line each and every day and makes a difference to others by guiding, listening, and teaching teamwork as his passions and goals. Stephen said that there are still people in his community and in the schools, who hold his transness against him, but progress is being made day to day.

As an ally to the T community, Wade Davis taught the audience, including me, that being an ally is not a passive role. He said, "Allies need to take *action*." They need to speak and be heard. He also said, "When you do not know about someone or his or her life, there is only one thing to do, which is to listen. This will lead to learning and acceptance, not judgment and denial. "

Jazz Jennings and her mom shared a variety of stories of their battle to allow Jazz to play competitive children's soccer and now high school tennis. It appeared that nothing was ever easy, but this family never gave up, and are an inspiration to us all.

ESPN Panel: Wade Davis, Stephen Alexander, Christina Kahrl, Chloie Johnson, Chris Mosier.

During Q&A and a question regarding the advantage of transwoman playing women's sports, I was able to relate to Christina's personal experience when she shared, "I have been on [drug therapy] HRT for 13 years now, and I cannot even open a jar. Why did they ever invent jars anyway?" I myself being on estrogen for five years get it. I can barely carry the grocery bags up the stairs now. I wouldn't have it be any different.

The bottom line: From childhood through college, for all amateur sports, and even professional sports, the rules for allowing trans people to belong and perform are inconsistent at best, and outlandish and ignorant at worst. Sports are a must for so many of us to keep our heads on straight in this increasingly complex world. Trans youth must be allowed to play and play equally and not singled out. Panels like this are just a start to point this out. There is still much work to do. We need to know: where will the children play?

There is another Cat Stevens song that leaves me with some hope.

> *Now I've been crying lately*
> *Thinking about the world as it is*
> *Why must we go on hating*
> *Why can't we live in bliss*
> *'Cause out on the edge of darkness*
> *There rides a peace train*
> *Oh, peace train take this country*
> *Come take me home again*
> *Oh, peace train sounding louder*
> *Glide on the peace train*
> *Come on the peace train*

– Cat Stevens, "Peace Train"

Chicken Is to Egg as Understanding Is to Acceptance

I started to wonder if the work I was so keen on doing, the teaching of understanding who we—trans people—are and how we feel, was the only path to gain acceptance. I toyed with the idea that perhaps there was another way, and then I came to realize that it should be flipped. If we follow the path of love rather than the path of fear, why wouldn't acceptance come first? I wondered...

Posted: 07/02/2015

Chicken is to egg.

It is hard to believe it was a decade ago that I applied to go back to school to pursue a master's degree in counselling at the tender age of 58. This was four years after the end of my 25-year marriage, when my inner battle with gender dysphoria was beginning to bubble over without any idea of how to deal with it.

I had some false starts with masters' programs earlier in my life. I got halfway through programs in Electrical Engineering and an MBA, which were both aborted for various reasons. Even thinking about a counselling degree, I had no idea or even intent that I would complete it or even dare think that I, with my own issues to deal with, could ever be of use to another person with their own issues. Nonetheless, I decided to apply for a program to, at the very least, see if I could figure out more about myself.

As I worked my way through the application and requirements, I was pleasantly surprised to see that there was no requirement to take GREs or any other standardized test that might be measuring some specific knowledge. However, there was a requirement to take something called the Miller Analogies. I had mixed feelings about this assessment, as I learned it was not something one could prepare for, but more provides a measure of overall general knowledge and perhaps interconnection between things. The application stated that acceptance decisions were not based on the actual score, but the school has found that people who do well on analogies are often able to be helpful in both understanding and communicating with a variety of clients.

This was my first learning experience in the program. It was a major learning even before I was accepted, and continued to be important as four years later I completed the program, and then for the past six years working with a variety of people.

This brings me to now, and the title of this blog:

Chicken is to egg

as

Understanding is to acceptance.

I think of these as a response to the question of, *what comes first?* I am certain that everyone has at least wrestled for some amount of time trying to answer whether the chicken or egg came first. Debates from evolutionists and creationists can go on forever and can either be fun or tedious depending on your own viewpoint.

This brings me to the second part of the analogy. What comes first: understanding or acceptance?

Even just a year ago, as I completed the manuscript of my book, *No! Maybe? Yes! Living My Truth*, I truly believed that if I could bring the reader into my own experience and feel what I have felt all my life, they could and would gain a better understanding of what it has been like being gender variant. If I could succeed in getting them to understand, my hope was that it would then be easier to lead to acceptance. Even my first blog here, back in February, was a response to the voices on ESPN radio, yelling that they do not understand anything about wanting to change gender, and I thought I was on the right track.

However, something in me changed over the last five to six months. The more I met and chatted with different people and had a chance to think about not only gender diversity, but diversity of all kinds—and this may be an uncountable number—I started to question whether I or anyone else really did need to understand everything before they could accept it. I wondered if I could accept first and then work on the understanding part as best I could.

This was a challenge for me. In my over 40 years as an engineer and engineering manager, taking things apart, working to break down structures and understanding every small detail in order to make sure things will work properly became my primary way of being in the world, both in and outside of my work environment. This was my go-to method, and even when it did not seem to be effective, I could not move off of it. In counselling school and after, it still took a great deal of effort to not allow this to be my primary framework. At long last, I believe I have been able to put this framework into background mode. At long last, I began to believe the following:

People are not things to be taken apart and put back together. People need to be accepted for who they truly are, and allowed to be on their own unique journey.

Perhaps I will recognize their journey immediately and either agree with it or not, but my opinion, or judgment on it does not give it value as right or wrong or good or bad. It has taken me a long, long time to get to this point of understanding. Perhaps it is because I am no longer hiding my truth, perhaps it my counselling experience, perhaps it my daily dose of estrogen, but it does not matter why, just that this feels so correct and so much better.

So, I will leave the question and analogy for you to work out for yourself. Which comes first? Acceptance or understanding?

For those of you who may have said, "I do not understand all this transgender stuff," and ignore it or reject it as something strange, different, or wrong, I suggest there may be another way to look at it. Understanding may not be the first step to take. Understanding may well come if you give it a chance. If you can choose the path of acceptance first, you may also allow that understanding to follow.

It took me a while, but I now know putting acceptance first is the better path.

No! Maybe? Yes! Not Just a Transgender Memoir

By Joan Brunwasser, Senior Editor, OpEdNews.com

I have learned to love the random messages people send me ever since my first book was published. One day I received an email from Joan Brunwasser, who said she was at one of her friends' house and saw my book there. It turned out, that her friend was also a friend of mine. Joan asked me if she could interview me for Op-ed news. I was surprised and honored by the request. It was a digital interview where she emailed a question and I emailed a response. Great fun. Having recieved permission to reprint the interview, here it is.

Posted 07/06/2015

Interview with author, Grace Anne Stevens

My guest today is Grace Anne Stevens, trainer, speaker and author of *No! Maybe? Yes! Living My Truth* [Graceful Change Press, 2015].

JB: Welcome to OpEdNews, Grace. Please tell our readers why you wrote this book.

GAS: Joan, thanks so much for inviting me to share with your readers. I look at my book as something much more than just a transgender memoir. Some people see it as a transgender story, some as a self-help book but, for me, it is really a love story—how I learned to love myself.

The "why" behind it really began in 2009 about a month after I shared with my adult children that I was transgender. At that time,

I had no idea where my journey was going to take me. A few months after, my youngest son, who was married, owned a house, and was living and teaching in Tucson, called me and said he was wrestling with not feeling he was living his true life. He stated that he did not want to be my age and realize he went down the wrong path!

This shocked me and made me realize that not living one's truth is not just an issue for transgender people, but really one that is present for all people everywhere, and perhaps, just perhaps, there was a mission for me to help teach about this. As I wrote this book in 2014, I felt it was part of this mission.

JB: I definitely want to discuss your mission, but first, let's talk about how you learned to love yourself—an essential task for each and every one of us. You transitioned at age 64. While I admittedly know little about transgender, it does seem quite late to make such a major life change. What took you so long?

GAS: Yes, that question, "what took so long?" was something that was in the back of my mind every day of my life as I managed to live in denial of all the feelings inside me of feeling "different" and "wrong" and having no idea how to reach self-acceptance and that there really was nothing wrong with me.

Getting married and raising three children kept me busy and occupied with responsibilities and what I "should be" and "should be doing" for over 25 years. It did a great but far from perfect job in holding me back from really having to face my truth of who I am. Even after I left my marriage of 25 years in 2001, it still took me another eight years to come to terms with the fact that I am a transsexual. Once I could say that and admit it to myself, then the work of deciding what to do about it began.

JB: So it sounds like a gradual process, rather than a sudden revelation. Repressing your feelings all that time can't have been good for you, and it must have affected your relationships with others. Can you talk about that, please?

GAS: For most of my life, I was not even aware of how much I was repressing my feelings. The reality is that I had them completely blocked. People often ask the question of what comes first among the three constructs of DO—BE—HAVE. I became very good at DOING and HAVING all the while blocking my sense of BEING. Without an honest sense of myself, I did not let myself feel. You are correct that without being able to access and communicate feelings, it did not allow me to be in any successful relationships with others, and, as I eventually learned, even with myself. I was in many relationships but when asked and even pressed as to what or how I felt, I would freeze, avoid, or even fabricate a response.

JB: So, how does one go from being frozen or out of touch to being more attuned to and in sync with one's inner workings? How did you? It can't have been easy.

GAS: I talk about this a lot in my book: about after leaving my marriage in 2001, going through what I call my "Existential Crisis"where I would come home from work each night and cry for hours, realizing that if I did not do something different (and I really did not know what that could be at the time), I would repeat everything all over again if I dared to look for new relationships.

The crying went on each night for a few weeks as I started to read, and somehow, and I am not certain how this occurred, I started to "play" with the feelings that were presenting to me. It was not easy, and I described it as being like the kid in the candy shop, tasting each new feeling. I started to share some of this with some people at work and with my kids, and it is still something I try to explore today.

JB: Once you eventually decided that transitioning was what you wanted to do, you had many tricky hurdles ahead of you: not the least being telling your adult children and colleagues. How did you prepare for that? Weren't you petrified?

GAS: It was the spring of 2009, about a year after I started to go out dressed as a woman, when I felt that I had to tell my kids. My thought process was that if anything ever happened to me when I was out dressed, I did not want my family to find out in a bad situation. At this time, I had no plan or idea that I would eventually transition but was on a path of exploration and really trying to understand all the forces that were always inside of me. The fear of calling a meeting, and then saying the words "I am transgender" was difficult but I knew it had to be done, as I was more petrified by them finding out without me telling them.

When I decided that I would transition, which occurred in late 2010, the hardest part in my decision process was the fear that my kids would abandon me. I am blessed and lucky that this never happened. I did force everyone in my family to go on a journey they never planned on, but we are still a family.

JB: You are incredibly lucky, Grace. I imagine that many people do not have such good fortune in that department. Let's talk a moment about the "collateral damage" when a person embarks on a journey like this. It's really hard to be mindful of others when you are in the midst of so much change and growth. What have you learned from your experience that could be helpful to someone else in a similar situation?

GAS: This is such a large and difficult subject. There is a saying that is used in the trans community:

You don't have choice in being transgender.

You do have a choice in what you do about it.

Even with that being said, it seems that many people will go from denial to ultimately reach some form of self-acceptance. Once this point is reached, when we want to share our discovery of our new sense of who we are, we want everyone to jump on board with us. This does not often occur, as we may have a hard time realizing that there are so many reasons that wanting this looks like we are self-centered and selfish and care only about ourselves. I tell people that when you are thinking about transitioning, you need to be prepared to lose everything and everyone in your life.

JB: That's harsh.

GAS: The choice of what one does about being transgender requires a careful balance of what I call the choice between "Being

ME" and "Being WE". Can one transition or not transition and keep all parts of their life in balance? There is not one simple answer or way to do this. Many relationships and families are torn apart. This is so sad. I hope that as more discussions like this appear, people will learn to understand and accept that being transgender is not a choice and not something that has an on/off switch.

JB: You were an engineer for many years; now you are a counselor and trainer; at one point, you were both engineer and counselor. How did getting this second degree and career play into your self-actualization?

GAS: I often cannot believe that while in a successful career as what might be described as a TYPE-A highly directive, in-charge engineering manager, I start to go down a path where I will sit down, build a relationship with people, listen carefully and learn to hold up a mirror with suggestions but not tell them how to live their lives.

In 2005, when I went to a group interview as part of the counseling program admitting process, the interviewer asked me why I wanted to become a counselor. I look back at my response in dismay: I said "I am an engineer and program manager, and I want to help fix people!" She nodded knowingly, and moved on to the next person. Somehow, they still admitted me and, class by class, I learned that counselors and therapists do not fix people!

The more I was taught, about the relationship between counselor and client as the primary part of the healing work, the more I found myself going inside to work on my internal relationship, which can be considered what you call self-actualization.

JB: Yes, it's quite a shift in perspective going from problem-solver to facilitator. Tell us, please, who you work with in your counseling and training and how that's going.

GAS: When I received my MA in Counseling Psychology in 2009, I chose to continue to work days in the tech world and also worked two to three nights each week at a substance abuse clinic where I interned. Over my six years at the clinic, I had both individual clients, and facilitated treatment groups. I found a great deal of excitement when I facilitated and taught the psycho-education groups for first offender drunk drivers. Here in Massachusetts, anyone with a first OUI violation is mandated to take a 32-hour alcohol education class. For the past six years, I have probably taught 400 to 500 people in these classes. I learned to teach the required curriculum of the state's program and add a good deal about relationships in these classes. I found that this part of "Grace's Curriculum" often had a strong impact on many of the attendees, as they got to learn more about themselves, rather than being told they were bad people for getting an OUI.

When my tech job was eliminated in 2013, I created a consulting company called Gender Variance Education and Training where I go into organizations to help trainings at all levels if and when someone chooses to transition gender in the workplace, a school, or organization. For a number of people, I may be the first trans person they have ever met, so it is important that I present as knowledgeable and professional.

Now, with another "reinvention" as an author, which is so exciting, I have also started a speaking business and hope to go into colleges and talk about living your true life, and authenticity, which is much more than just an issue in the transgender community.

Each day is a new adventure and is very exciting.

JB: I like your attitude! How did your own transition in your workplace go? How did you prepare your colleagues?

GAS: Thanks. I had taken four weeks off from my tech job to have and recuperate from Facial Feminization Surgery (FFS), and they held a training session for about 200 people the week before I returned. I wrote a six-page letter to give a personal view about my journey and also provided a frequently asked questions sheet (FAQ) within it (a copy of this and other letters I wrote are at the end of my book). The day I returned to work as Grace, I remember parking my car, reaching the door and momentarily freezing before I opened it and walked up the stairs to my office, which had a brand new nameplate on it that said Grace Stevens.

For the first time, I left my purse under my desk and went to my boss's office to introduce myself. It was amazing that first week. So many people came by and told me how brave I was and how great I looked. The most amazing thing was a woman I did not know came by and shared that she was trans but no one here knew this! Many women came by, invited me to lunch and told me it was so much easier to talk with me than it used to be.

It was a large campus and not everyone went to the trainings, so there were a few awkward/funny moments as time went on but, overall, my transition at work was a great experience and I had many teaching moments.

JB: I'm so glad. It most certainly didn't have to go so well and all workplaces are not as supportive. How does the recent Supreme Court decision supporting same sex marriage play into all this or doesn't it?

GAS: The SCOTUS decision, although not related to transgender rights or even an inkling about gender identity and expression, is of major importance to the idea of just letting people be who they are and let them live and love whoever they want, with all the rights and blessings of the government which, we learned as youngsters, is instituted of, for, and by the people.

What is much more important is all the great work being done in the present administration supporting trans rights and removing any restrictions on transgender health services from insurance coverages for federal agencies and suppliers. This is the work of many great organizations that is culminating in saving the lives of many people. There is hope for many who have been hopeless for so long.

JB: That is important. I wasn't aware of that. Your book is out now. What kind of feedback are you getting?

GAS: The feedback on my book has been wonderful. I was not certain whether the framework of telling my story from the voices of the little girl and little boy that have always been inside me would resonate with people, but it appears to have done so both inside and outside of the trans community. Since I also jumped between my personal story and what I learned along the way, it is very different than and something more than most memoirs.

Within the trans community, feedback has been that I have articulated some feelings that people did not know how to explain. Also, numerous people have bought multiple copies to give to their friends and even therapists to help explain what they are feeling. This is amazing and so fulfilling. Outside the trans community, I have received much feedback that my journey to return to school at age 58 has inspired people that it is never too late to reinvent yourself.

Getting this feedback is like being in a great and wonderful dream....I keep pinching myself to see if I am awake!

JB: Lovely. What haven't we talked about yet?

GAS: My journey for so many decades was ruled by confusion, shame, and fear. I have been blessed and lucky all through my life, although not without the daily challenges of life and relationships, both good and bad.

It was not easy to come to terms and understand the confusion of feeling I was not really a man, but once I reached self-acceptance and was able to let go of the shame and fear, I found that I was able to open up so much to myself, my feelings, and those of others, in a way I could not before.

I learned so much from my kids that thinking we needed to be a certain way for other people holds all of us back from really living our true lives, and if and when we finally do live our truth, most people do not look at it as being selfish, but surprisingly, look at it as being courageous! I hope to inspire everyone to live with this courage!

JB: Thanks so much for talking with me, Grace. It was fun, and I learned a lot along the way.

GAS: My pleasure, Thanks so much.

I Know Someone Who Knows Someone Who...

I was still thinking about acceptance. The statistic that only 8 per-cent of the population knew someone who was trans was giving me an unpleasant feeling in the pit of my stomach, and I was wondering how to talk about it. The engineer parts of me started working on the geo-metric progressions of six degrees. It led to this article

Posted: 07/07/2015

Do you remember the old game called Six Degrees of Kevin Bacon? You know, name any actor and try to connect in the fewest hops of what movie they were in with someone who ultimately was in a movie with Kevin Bacon.

The entire game was based on a concept called six degrees of sepa-ration, which posits that any two people on earth are fewer than six acquaintance links apart.

This made me think about the recent survey report that only about 8 percent of the population knows someone who is transgender. I know that my own personal world does not fairly represent the coun-try as a whole, but when I go out to teach or speak, I ask the question and often see 20 to 30 percent or more hands go up.

I do believe that knowing someone who is transgender goes a long way to acceptance and understanding—and for those who have been following some of my writing, you know that I think the acceptance can come first. So the question started to swim around my mind: How far can the separation of acquaintance links be in order to foster and grow transgender acceptance?

If you know someone who is trans, have you ever been in a conversation with a friend, a co-worker, even a stranger in a line somewhere, where you got to say, "I know someone who is transgender, and they are so courageous and happy being their true self!" Have you ever heard someone then repeated it as, "I know someone who knows someone who is transgender and...."

– ☼ –

Once again, I will state that we are all unique, just like snowflakes! There is no one way, no right way to *be* transgender. Just because you may know someone who is transgender that does not mean you know everyone who is transgender. There are trans people in the public. Some do great things, while some do not! Some are heroes, while some are not. Some are highly visible and some hide themselves and their past, which all is fine. Almost all of them, all of us, have gone through an internal battle to understand and hopefully accept ourselves as best we possibly can. No two of us have taken the same path to live our truth. Each one of us has had the courage to move forward and possibly lose everything and everyone that is near and dear to us. Yes, each one of us reached this crossroad!

When you know someone who is trans, someone who has had an incredible challenge in his or her life and was incredibly brave enough to face their internal challenge in spite of not mapping to society's expectations. The more people you meet and get to know, the more you will realize that they are not that much different than you, but perhaps their specific challenges are. Perhaps it is the millions of trans people that are facing their challenges who can teach everyone to face their own and live their true life, whatever that may be.

– ☼ –

Six degrees of separation does not seem so far away. Neither does even two degrees or three degrees of separation. The media reported that over 17 million people saw the Diane Sawyer/Jenner interview this past April. If each of those people told two people they know a trans person and then they told two people, there would be over 150 million people at two degrees of separation. This may sound silly, but that is the power of the media and the way we see knowledge being spread.

Most of us, not just trans people, want to live our lives as our true selves. We need people in our life to accept us as someone who had a challenge that we did not ask for but have learned to deal with. We are not crazy, impaired, or doing anything wrong.

We are trying to end our internal six degrees of separation, and bring together all those parts and aspects inside of us that have been battling for many years and bring them all together as the person we truly are.

I bet you are too!

What Makes a Hero?

I know, I know. I thought I was done reflecting on the Jenner Journey. It was not that simple! I was wondering if I was sticking my head in the sand, as I tried to stay out of the fray that was pretty rampant across the transgender community. I knew how I felt, but it really was not the focus of my message. Once again, I found a need to position my thoughts in a way to be thoughtful and considered, and not strictly critical. I searched for the teaching moment.

Posted: 07/09/2015

Is it really less than three months since Diane Sawyer's Jenner interview aired? So much has happened in the past three months, including the world's introduction to Caitlyn Jenner. It seems that there is not a day that goes by without not one, but multiple mentions of Caitlyn in the media. Some days it is as simple as what she is wearing; some days it is a new trailer for the not-yet-started reality show; some days it is new blog that she has written, and on some days it can be all of these events.

On July 15, she will also be seen on the ESPN *ESPYs* as the recipient of the Arthur Ashe Courage Award. To me, it makes no difference if you are a fawning fan of the Jenner juggernaut or are fanning yourself from Jenner fatigue; Caitlyn has created an awareness of gender variance far and wide in a manner never before seen or even dreamed about. Perhaps the legendary athlete is still dreaming of setting new records, which may well be what she knows how to do best!

I have been thinking a lot about the idea of giving Caitlyn an award for courage. She is certainly neither the first, nor will she be the last, transgender person who will come out and transition, whether publicly or privately. Each and every one has exhibited the very same courage that Caitlyn is being awarded for. The day I returned to work when I transitioned, there were dozens of people who came to my office to tell me how brave and courageous I was. This became increasingly difficult for me to hear, as not for a single moment did I feel brave or courageous about transitioning. I felt I had no choice if I wanted to find any internal peace. I am pretty sure that Caitlyn must have had similar feelings—almost everyone I know in the transgender community has shared something similar.

The only way I can make sense of this award is that it is not about Caitlyn. Caitlyn is a *symbol*, and a larger than life symbol at that. Almost 40 years ago. Jenner was a record-setting Olympic champion, becoming a symbol of American sports dominance, so perhaps this will be familiar territory for her. Her history leads me to believe that the symbol status she obtained in the past was undertaken with some reluctance. With her *Vanity Fair* photo shoot, I suspect this has now changed.

I myself am just a few years older than Caitlyn, and transitioned four years ago at the age of 64. I understand the excitement. I remember my shopping spree before I returned to work, and the semiplanned fashion show I was performing each day for the first month (or more) of my transition. For the past six years, I have been a board member of The Tiffany Club of New England, one of the oldest transgender support groups, and have been meeting and supporting many people on their gender variant journeys—where no two have been the same.

As a college student back in the sixties, I remember the discussions about Marshall McLuhan's teaching: "The medium is the message." In his classic book, *Understanding Media: The Extensions of Man* (1964) McLuhan proposed that a medium affects the society in which it plays a role not only by the content delivered over the medium, but by the characteristics of the medium itself.

In our present day world of instant communication, could it be that Caitlyn Jenner has become a "medium," as we have witnessed that a single cover picture of her seems to have had a huge impact on our society? Has she once again become a symbol, just as she was 40 years ago, and again the content has perhaps less meaning than even she desires? I can feel for Caitlyn, I can empathize for her, as I have myself walked in her shoes. I know the shame, the fear, the confusion of hiding for so many decades.

For most of us, the time of transition is the deeply personal work of rediscovery and reinvention. It is hard enough to do it in private, as these discoveries are often not quick in coming to our awareness. Doing this in public takes either a certain courage or bravado, and I sincerely hope that in Caitlyn's desire to "do good" it is the former.

I have shared with my friends that after almost 50 years, I have been rereading Frank Herbert's masterpiece, *DUNE*. (For those not familiar with the book, the hero is a young man who becomes the hero, the messiah figure, also known as Muad'Dib—the one who points the way.) Here is a quote from it that I believe is worth sharing:

> *Greatness is a transitory experience. It is never consistent. It depends in part upon the myth-making imagination of humankind. The person who experiences greatness must have a feeling for the myth he is in. He must reflect what is projected upon him. And he must have a strong sense of the sardonic. This is what uncouples him from belief in his own pretensions. The sardonic is all that permits him to move within himself. Without this quality, even occasional greatness will destroy a man.*
>
> **—from "Collected Sayings of Muad'Dib" by the Princess Irulan**

Quote from *DUNE* by Frank Herbert.

Sometimes our society needs a hero. Sometimes our society needs a symbol.

The hero may be the leader we desperately want to follow without doing our own work. The symbol is what makes us go inside to question what and who we really are.

I am not certain what role Caitlyn fulfills for each person, whether they are trans or not. My hope is that she allows each person to go inside and question who they really are, and help to inspire each of us to be the hero of our own life!

Learning to Say Thank You

I was now five-plus months in, writing these blogs. Some weeks the ideas were jumping to be put on paper, and some weeks I searched for inspiration. This one was in the latter category that seemed to appear out of real life.

Posted: 07/14/2015

There is always another stretch!

I learned this from many of the growth seminars I attended over the past decade. Certainly, transitioning gender was a mighty stretch for me, my friends, and my family. In many ways, this is now old news, and each day is a new adventure, which provides another chance to stretch and grow.

Last Saturday night was a grand time at The Tiffany Club of New England (TCNE) annual BBQ. TCNE is one of the oldest transgender support groups and for over 30 years has provided a facility where gender variant people can come and meet others like themselves for friendship and support. With weekly open houses it is fairly unique in the transgender community, and over the past three decades has made a difference in many lives, mine included.

After I was finished grilling up the burgers, dogs, chicken, and veggies for close to 30 people, I had a chance to get some food myself and then chat with some of the folks present. It was then that a new learning entered my awareness.

One of the club's newer members, Shawna and I started to chat.

She kindly said, "Grace, you really look nice tonight. You look nicer than usual."

I froze! Have you ever had that moment when you are not sure whether you were receiving a compliment or maybe getting some kind of passive-aggressive "diss?" I am pretty aware with all the hiding and protecting that I have done for so much of my life it has been almost impossible for me to take in a compliment, and even if I could take it in, what in the world would I do or respond to it? That freeze moment that I experienced, which to the outside world may be one to two seconds, internally seemed like hours and hours of internal debate.

"What did I hear?" one of my internal voices cried out. Another voice yelled that she heard Shawna say that she thought I usually look pretty bad, while another was pleading everyone to slow down and stay present. "She said you looked nice, just stay with that," the voice continued.

I have been through these internal conversations so many times before and most often that angry and pissed off voice usually did not wait for any other thoughts and lashed out with, "Oh, you mean I usually look bad," comment. But not this night! The voice pleading to slow down seemed to get heard and what came out of my mouth was a real and sincere, "Thank you so much!"

While this only took second or so, I was focusing inside me, and I did not notice the similar look on Shawna's face indicating that she, too, had frozen as soon as she spoke to me. Once I said thanks, she looked right at me for a second and shared that she immediately felt she had said the wrong thing. There was an internal dialogue going on in her head, and she was so hoping that she had not hurt my feelings by indicating I did not look good previously to this evening. She said she did not mean to say anything negative but just wanted to compliment me. I shared with her that my internal voices immediately went to that negative space, but perhaps for one of the first times in my life, I was able to slow down the internal conversation and process the compliment. We then had an incredible conversation about how easy it is for us to go to the dark places rather than the ones that shine.

I don't know if this is the socialization that is different between boys and girls growing up, or socialization of people who may be hiding parts of their true selves from everyone around them, or something else entirely. I do know that for most of my life I would live in the paradox of wanting acknowledgments and compliments and if they ever came my way—and I do know that many have—I would instantaneously reject them in such a way that would make the giver so sorry that they even bothered. My desire to want to belong, want to be seen, wanting and needing to be valued and valuable, was triggering the don't dare get too close to me parts that would react without thinking and push that giver as far away as possible.

Since my transition it has still been hard for me to work with these parts, and letting them know it is OK to receive a compliment and just say thank you. Whether people say I am brave or courageous, or just look nice it has been hard to take in. It really is!

However, this Saturday night I became aware of something new. There are no other hooks or commitments involved. I am open and free and pushing other people away in fear of finding out who I truly am, no longer has any purpose.

At long last I am learning to say thank you. It is pretty cool.

Now, on to my next stretch.

How about you?

(Oh, and a big heartfelt thank you for reading my blogs.)

Home Is Where the Heart Sings

Another time traveling experience that I shared. The old songs still take me on flights to another time. However, now, I have very much learned to enjoy these journeys.

Posted: 07/21/2015

I make no apologies! I have already talked about the fact that I seem to time travel a bit. My brain will wander to other lands and times—some people call it daydreaming, but whatever it is, it is wonderful!

When I go walking at the town track each morning, I plug into my music library and before I know it I am taking another trip. The other morning as I scrolled though my choices and made my album selection, I had a different kind of experience. Have you ever realized that in a song that you have known for years, you may never have really listened, I mean deeply listened, to the words and the meaningin it? The other morning I was listening to Donovan…

Everybody who read the Jungle Book
Knows that Riki Tiki Tavi's a mongoose who kills snakes
When I was a young man I was led to believe
There were organizations to kill my snakes for me
IE, the church, IE, the government, IE, the school
But when I got a little older I learned how to kill them myself

– Donovan, "Riki Tiki Tavi"

Oh my, I thought. It sure has taken me a long time to realize I am the only one who can kill my snakes. Then he went on...

People walking around, they don't know what they're doing
They been lost so long, they don't know what they're looking for
Well, I know what I'm looking for but I just can't find it
I guess I gotta look inside of myself some more

– Donovan, "Riki Tiki Tavi"

It also has taken me decades to look inside myself and accept I am transgender. When I truly started to look inside myself, I also found something else that was hidden and covered in a very hard shell for so long. This was my heart. I have found over the past six years or so, as I have worked on my own self-acceptance, I have been able to chip away at that shell that was covering my heart for so many decades. This has been and still is hard work! As Donovan sang, I was lost for so long, and was looking in all the wrong places for what I was looking for...and only I could kill my snakes.

In 2011 when I transitioned I did not know who Grace was, and how she/I would present in the world on a daily basis. I knew I needed help and was lucky enough to find an image consultant to help me discover so much more about me. She helped me with my makeup and my colors, and a new affirmation, and took me on a shopping spree where she taught me one of the most important lessons I have learned in my life. As she brought outfit after outfit for me to try on, if I had even the smallest questioning frown, she demanded I take it off immediately and move on. She said, "Each thing you wear *must* make your heart sing!" For two hours I was trying on clothes and listening for the music inside of me. When I heard no music that outfit was rejected. There were different songs that I could hear with different outfits too. I learned so much from that experience.

There is an old saying, *home is where the heart is*. When my heart was covered in a hard shell, I never felt at home in my own body. The music I heard outside of me never resonated inside of me, and the music inside of me was so muffled and faint it could not get out. As I chipped away the hard shell, and looked inside, accepted myself, and found my heart, I could start to hear the songs in my heart, and I learned that the songs are there for much more than just picking out clothes. They are available if we live from our heart. I now have this plaque on my wall.

Do What Makes Your Heart Sing

A favorite wall plaque.

It took me a long time to learn to operate from this place. Sometimes there is a lot I learn from time traveling.

I love it when I hear the songs that are coming from inside me now. It does not matter if they are old songs or new ones. I love them all the same. I know that each day can be a new adventure. When I go shopping for new clothes or chose a new adventure I am learning not only to look inside but also to listen inside for the music that is there. When I hear a song I know I am home, as I have learned that:

Home is where the heart sings!

Have you chosen to stand up and dance to the song in your heart?
- Grace Anne Stevens

Song in your heart.

Maine-lining

There was a bit of an inner battle going on. I was going on vacation and thought that I would also skip writing during that week. A part of me was upset and felt I must continue on the weekly writing schedule. This inner battle still occurs. I guess I still have some inner work to do.

Posted: 07/29/2015

There are some habits that are really hard to break.

For my BFF and me our summer vacation to Maine is one of them, and it is that time of year once again. When we think of Maine, we think of bikes and beaches, lighthouses and lobsters. We are the ones who stay on the coast not the woods, the white waters, or the lakes, although we are wondering if we can break our present habit and expand in the future.

However, four years ago, when I transitioned, this habit was tested mightily!

My book *No! Maybe? Yes! Living My Truth* is dedicated to my BFF Tessa, and I wrote:

We said our goodbyes when I transitioned, but they did not stick, as we both learned that the meaning of true friendship was more important than my changing gender.

Not that this was an easy process. I transitioned in April of 2011 when I had Facial Feminization Surgery. We were not certain that we would take our annual summer vacation in Maine as we were playing everything out day to day. We had the hotel reserved, and I was prepared to, although with thoughts full of anxiety, go on vacation by myself.

– ☼ –

Make no mistake about it; transitioning gender will test each and every relationship in your life. As we come to terms with the relationship with ourselves, we ask everyone who knows us, who cares about us, who loves us, to go deeply inside and ask themselves what our transition means to them first, and us a distance second. Although we know how hard our journey may have been, we often have no idea how difficult the journeys we have asked all these people to go on also, and there may be no way for us to help them, as they are the only ones who can find the truth in their hearts about the relationship.

– ☼ –

The hotel was reserved in my old name, so that was the first thing to change. Tessa did not come in with me when I did this. We went to the beach and this was also new for me in how to dress for the beach — yes, I was full time but still had male anatomy. Both of us were self-conscious, so it was a bit uncomfortable. The mornings biking were fine as we were pretty much on our own, but anytime we were in crowds, and for dinners, she thought people were looking and pointing at us. By the end of the second day, she no longer wanted to go out in crowds, and we tended to stay off by ourselves. When we left we debated whether to hold the room for another year, as it was not the best of vacations. We did, but had no idea what the next year would be like.

The following summer trip occurred after I had another round of surgeries—gender reassignment and breast augmentation. For me swimsuits were no longer an issue, and I was excited to go to the beach. It was a little easier for Tessa but she still got triggered a few times when we were walking on the street and she thought people were pointing at us.

I don't know who has changed more over the past four years, her or me, but even though she tells me there are times she is a little uncomfortable, we now go anywhere and interact with people in stores and on the street just as any people would do. Certainly I am more and more comfortable in my own skin, but it seems that Tessa's journey to being comfortable in public with me may have been a more difficult journey than mine. Our friendship kept us going even through difficult times. I made no demands on her. I was there and understood and accepted her discomfort, and would follow her if she felt she/we needed to isolate to make her feel better.

It has been four years since my transition and our friendship has survived. The concern of me being me no longer seems to be a potential embarrassment to her, and she tells me she is no longer worried about the potential judgment of other people. Perhaps it is that there is more awareness of transgender people, or perhaps I may be less obviously a transgender person. Unless someone recognizes me—the whole idea of being "read" is so beyond me—but with my book and blogging and interviews—I am becoming an open public transgender woman. What is more likely is that Tessa, too, has changed and evolved as a person and has become more comfortable in her skin, her choices, and her friendships.

We said our goodbyes in 2011, but old habits are hard to change, the goodbyes were ignored, although not easily. We still are looking forward to bikes and beaches, lighthouses and lobsters. Oh, and that habit we had for a while of each of us having anxiety, well that habit has been broken. That's a good thing!

**Biking with my son at El Tour de Tucson,
pre-transition November 2009.**

Grace getting ready to bike in Maine, August 2014.

Denial, Betrayal, Abandonment, and Other Monsters Under the Bed

There were so many thoughts running through my mind. They seemed to all exist and all want to be chatted about, and I struggled how to make them fit together. So many things that we fear! Somehow the idea that these fears are monsters started to jell in my thoughts. Yes, they were monsters, and they were hiding and would sneak up on us whenever they could.

Posted: 08/04/2015

It is said that by the time we are seven years old our prefrontal cortex is pretty much wired to the rest of our brain. It is around this time that most of us begin to understand that there really are not monsters that live under our beds.

Or are there?

– ☼ –

It wasn't much later than when I was seven I knew that there was a monster still lurking under my bed. I knew that I could never tell anyone about it, because by that time everyone knew that monsters didn't exist. This was long past those days when I was four or five and loved those Sunday mornings when I would watch my father shave his pencil thin mustache and he let me use the Gillette safety razor with no double-sided blade in it. I was going to be just like dad!

But a few years later, I was being drawn to mom's closet, and I could not stop staring at her dresses. One day when no one was home I tried one on. Of course, it was way too large on me. Well, you know this story... but now the monster was loose. I could never tell anyone about this. This little pup of a monster was called *denial,* and over the years it learned so much.

I thought I was a cross-dresser for so many years as I snuck and hid the times I dressed up in women's clothes. I did this when I was single, married, and then single again. That *denial* monster grew and grew. He became so strong he was even denying that I was not really a cross-dresser, but something quite different. It took me until I was 62 years old to tame that monster and admit I am a transsexual.

It may sound strange that I consider myself lucky that my marriage ended long before I tamed the *denial* monster. I have many friends in long-term marriages working on their *denial* monsters and I hear stories of their partners being taken over by their own *betrayal* monster. I have a sense that the *denial* and *betrayal* monsters are mortal enemies. It is a shame how hard it is for people in relationship to tame these monsters. I doubt that my own marriage would have survived this battle way back when. These battles leave so much destruction in their path. It seems that only a lucky few are able to survive. I hope this difficulty for understanding and acceptance changes.

When one feels betrayed and lied to, there is a clear sense of being violated. How often we get into relationship and believe we know the other person, their thoughts, their feelings, even their secrets. How we believe they will always be there for us, just as we know they are right now! Our own small *denial* monsters let us believe this lie because we think it makes our life so much better. Even if we know we keep secrets from our partner, this matters not, as it is the secrets we keep from ourselves that are at the root of all the problems. However, when we see through our own lies to ourselves—and most of us eventually get there sooner or later, as we tame our internal *denial* beastie, the war of the monsters begins and often it beckon a new monster that has been hiding under the bed for many, many years. This monster is called *abandonment*. This is one of those two-headed beasts that are so hard to slay. When our partner turns out to be different or changing from the picture we have emblazoned in our mind, this monster attack us first with the feeling of being lost, forgotten, displaced and joins with *betrayal* to make you question everything that occurred before. It frees our anger, which feeds the other head of *abandonment,* which then follows through with yelling or silence…and threatening (oh, such a variety of threats are possible here) and it is interesting to see these two heads breathing fire in all directions.

How often all is lost, when the monsters win!

— ☼ —

I think that if we learn that these monsters are real, we can take away their power. If we know their names, and how they try to control us, they will lose their power. When we stop lying to ourselves, when we accept all, then our relationships with ourselves and others may change over time. When we love unconditionally without fear or neediness, when we believe we are strong enough to face all of our own monsters, then the ones we named and all the others under our beds will no longer be able to hurt us.

It is not easy to tame or slay our monsters. They sneak up when we are not looking and sometimes we do not even know they have trapped us. But we can succeed! Even if we were knocked down, or singed around the edges, we can recover and grow in many new and surprising ways and directions.

Change is not a bad thing. Especially when we can change our monsters into peaceful companions!

The Lost and Found

I found myself going inside—deeply inside, and willing to share this story. If I say I have no secrets, I have found I need to go inside to see what I still may be hiding from myself.

Posted: 08/11/2015

For so many years I had no idea how lost I really was. I think this may not only be true for many trans folk, but it might be true for almost everyone too!

By all outward appearances, I was pretty successful. I was married for 25 years, raised three fabulous kids in an upper middle class suburb and thought I was living the American dream of the boomer generation that I was part of.

Yet, I knew there was something missing, as I knew that all of this was not enough. No, not really that it was not enough; because after all, it was plenty and more than most ever get to have. It was something very different. There was always the inner battle with gender variance. I was aware of that seemingly forever, although—with various degrees of difficulty—was able to keep it in check.

This all seemed to be working. Until…

My marriage ended after 25 years. The details of this are not important here. My internal battle with gender was a total secret and never, never, an open issue, although what it was doing to me internally at the time, I had no words to describe.

— ☼ —

I was already lost in elementary school. By the second grade, I did not know where I fit in. I did not have any friends in my classes that I would see after school. The boys seemed to talk about playing ball, and I had no idea how to do that. Growing up in a two-room apartment in a big building in Brooklyn, ball playing to me was playing "hit the penny" with a pink rubber ball. This is where you put a penny on a crack between two "boxes" on the sidewalk, and you try to hit the penny with the ball. My father kept making fun of me saying I threw like a girl—while he never taught me how to throw. This made me mad on so many levels.

In third grade, the boys played softball after school and one day I was asked to join them. I had no idea what I was doing. I learned what it was like to be the last person picked as sides were chosen. This made me mad on so many levels.

Inside me, there was so much anger, and I felt so lost. I had no idea where I belonged. I did not know how to play with the boys. I just wanted to watch TV, but I had to belong with them, I really did. But there were the days with mom's dresses too. I was so confused, so lost. All this made me mad on so many levels.

Over time, I learned to play ball with the boys. I learned to grab the ball first and lead, and worked myself up from being the last pick to the one who was team captain, who did the picking. I belonged there with the boys, but inside I had lost so much of myself. I led most of my life not really knowing my true self, fighting what I thought was the good fight, having a successful career, getting married, raising a family. Deep down, I knew I had lost not only the sense of who I was, but also the ability to feel. I could fake it, and certainly did for so long, but it was only after my marriage ended that I stopped blaming others for what I lacked, and dared to look for what I lost so long ago.

Some may call it courage. To the best of my knowledge that word never entered my mind. Looking back on that time, it felt more like being trapped in a locked room and there was only one door to get out. I had to go deeply inside to escape the trap I found myself in. There was no other choice!

— ☼ —

So many parts of me inside were broken. I had no idea! Some were hiding, some were crying, one kept her back turned to me and refused to answer when I called to her. I stepped closer but what looked like a very large dog started to growl and I backed away. A box in the corner had a faded sign on it, and as I got closer, I made out the word "feelings." I took a quick look behind me and knew there was no turning back. This box was overflowing as I started to gently pick through piece after piece. As I rummaged through this box, there was a flood of tears falling from my eyes. I knew these were falling both inside of me and outside too. Some of the pieces were damp, some were ice cold, and some made a gentle purring sound as I picked them up as if they were happy to be found and held. I took a few of these with me, as it was time for me to go back to my "real" world.

— ☼ —

So much has changed for me since I discovered that place. I am no longer lost, as I have found so many of my lost parts and have chosen to live as my authentic self. There is no trapped room with only a single way out. I am free in the world!

I've gone back to my Lost and Found many times since that day. I know there are still many lost pieces of me to discover and become friends with. I don't really have a plan as to when I go, or what I am looking for, but find so much joy—yes, a feeling—in each new discovery of a lost part of me. I hope that I do not lose any other parts of me as I continue my journey, but if I do, now I know where to find them.

Second Chances

To be on this journey I am on, I wake up each day full of gratitude. The day may be easy and wonderful, or the day may be difficult and I may want to run away. However, I never lose track how blessed I am to have been able to live my truth.

Posted: 08/17/2015

*Live as if you were living a second time and
as though you had acted wrongly the first time.*

– Viktor Frankl, Man's Search for Meaning

Last week I was excited to celebrate my birthday. On the record it was number 68. Off the record, I like to think that 68 is the new 28, but perhaps I'm fooling myself. Even though I transitioned at the age of 64, I don't believe anything I've done in my life was a mistake, and I am in deep gratitude that I now have a second chance to live my life in a manner that is true to how I see myself. Before I transitioned, I seemingly traveled through my life in a cloud, and the lens I viewed the world through was always out of focus. Perhaps that might be a definition of dysphoria for some. I know it was for me

Second chances can mean lots of different things to different people. I love the way Viktor Frankel talks about living your life as if you get to correct mistakes—or as he says, "acting wrongly," that you've made before. To me this is the ultimate second chance. However, finding one's true meaning of life and actually living it does not necessarily mean that you've made a mistake before you reach this point. I am aware of people in and out of the transgender community that may feel that their lives before they chose to live authentically, was living in error or a mistake. I am not one of them, as I treasure each moment in my life, whether it was full of pleasure or full of challenge. I own it all; the good—the bad—the consequences and the rewards. Sometimes it takes a while to figure out all of one's life puzzle pieces and get the picture right! There is no need to judge the past, present, or future. This is true for ourselves and for others.

It's not often that you get a second chance!

— ☼ —

I suspect that not many people have heard of Viktor Frankl and his classic book, *Man's Search for Meaning*. The book that was birthed out of the horrors of World War II German concentration camps, as a young Frankl learned the power of hope and love, and that each person has their unique mission. However, I also suspect that almost all of us, will ask the question, "What is the meaning of our life?" I know I have, and I have learned from Frankl, when he states:

...the meaning of life differs from man to man, from day to day, and from hour to hour. What matters, therefore, is not the meaning of life in general but rather the specific meaning of a person's life at a given moment.

About a month ago, it was late evening as I watched Jimmy Fallon return from his finger injury. As he discussed his experience, I must admit that I almost fell off of my couch when Fallon discussed reading Frankl's book as he was in the hospital for 10 days recovering. The always-smiling Fallon said that almost losing his finger allowed his self-reflective parts to ask himself what his life is about, and his answer was that his mission was to entertain people. I wonder if anyone in his audience decided to get the book.

Jimmy Fallon Explains His Finger Injury

Fallon talks about Frankl. (*Tonight Show*)

You can listen to the video of Jimmy Fallon on YouTube here: https://youtu.be/CztT_pBFQv8.)

— ☼ —

I first read *Man's Search for Meaning* in 2006. I was divorced, struggling with my own gender dysphoria and desperately searching for meaning and hope wherever I could find it. It is not an easy read but it planted many seeds of understanding in me—some that took me a few years to digest and act on to find and live my truth and find my mission to help teach people to discover their own authentic life, whatever that may look like for each person.

I talk about living in the present and being aware that change happens in every moment. I have learned much from Viktor Frankl, and perhaps you may too. Life changes in each moment. Frankl eloquently sums it up:

Ultimately, man should not ask what the meaning of life is, but rather he must recognize that it is he who is asked. In a word, each man is questioned by life; and only he can answer to life by answering for his own life; to life, he can only respond by being responsible.

– ☼ –

Frankl teaches us the power of love and hope. I believe I have made the most of my second chance. I have learned from Frankl—I am responsible for me and my choices. No one else! Perhaps 68 is the new 28, but I know that last week, as I celebrated my birthday with most of my kids and grandkids, that love and hope is forever present in my life. You know, in this moment, that is certainly meaning enough for me.

It's not often that you get a second chance!

Treasure your second chances when they come, or even be responsible and make them happen yourself!

Labels and Boxes

One of my missions is to "break the binary." I realize that this is more complicated than it sounds. It is so human to want to have boxes and categories to place things in. We argue that this makes it easier to understand. Unfortunately this is, at best, only a partial truth. So perhaps my mission needs to include: "Break the boxes!"

Posted: 08/24/2015

What's in a name? That which we call a rose
By any other name would smell as sweet;

– William Shakespeare, *Romeo and Juliet*

No surprise here, *Words have power!*

No, I am not just talking about those magical spells in the Potterverse that so many of us have learned to escape to, but I am talking about those every day comments that can enhance or tear apart one's very soul.

I am talking about some simple words and phrases that we use every day that have the power to make or break our connection with others.

"I understand," are the words that will bring connection and comforting warmth.

"You don't understand," bring the icy bards that separate and threaten connection in so many ways.

So much power in so few words!

– ☼ –

To me, being human is quite magical in itself, whether or not we can control mysterious forces to cast spells on others. We have the magic of language, which when I was a young one, was taught to me that this is what separated us from the rest of the animal kingdom. I did accept this idea way back then but after so much time, I begin to wonder about its truth.

We have the magic of emotions and feelings. For some of us this is a source of ongoing wonder and joy, yet for others it may seem that we are ruled by dark forces we cannot control, and fight against with all our might. I know what this is like as for much of my life most of my energies were spent to draw a curtain over all the feelings that would bubble up in me. I was so afraid that if I shared what was inside of me, I would never hear the magical warmth of "I understand!"

Again, when I was a young one, I was taught that there were those two boxes that people fit in. There was the mostly Blue box that was labeled "male" and the Pinkish box that was labeled "female." It was so simple, and there were no other possibilities. When you were born you were placed in a box and given a label and that was that!

For anyone who dared to creep or crawl their way out of the box they were placed in—even if they just wanted to explore—there would be so many voices, so many forces pushing them back—some starting out gently but invariably getting stronger and less gentle with the messages always saying you need to go back where you belong, and "You don't understand!" For those who were exploring, their internal voices were struggling to yell out, "No! It is you who do not understand!" Some of those internal voices were also struggling themselves to understand why they did not feel right in the box they were put in, but were so afraid to say this to anyone.

In a world where gender is thought to be a binary construct of male and female, those of us who do not fit in the simple constructs, whether we feel we are in the wrong box or the boxes are insufficient to describe ourselves, often go through a life of confusion, fear, shame and struggle. It is a challenge to ever find the words to express what we feel.

For so many, it is so much easier to place things and people in a box with a simple label on it. It does not matter if the label is correct or even if what is in the box may change over time. This requires work for us and even the risk of exploring our own feelings—and there may be danger in that!

Sometimes our human gifts of language and feelings are not compatible. Can I ever express my true sense of being me to another person? I am pretty certain that is a desire we all have. Can I know you? Can you know me?

– ☼ –

Even within the transgender community there appears to be ongoing changes in language, in labels and in boxes on how we describe and communicate what our feelings are inside. I get it! There are times when knowing where things belong is quite useful. Being able to organize, list, and categorize are most often considered to be valuable skills for both young and old. Losing this ability is often a warning sign of mental decline.

Sometimes we even need to have a label for ourselves so we can understand where we are, where we belong, how to share our feelings. This is hard and by no means ever exact. It may be a struggle to find the words, but I wonder if it is ever worthy of a fight about it?

Juliet knew the truth that the names—the words did not matter. Her family, culture, and society did not, and her story ended as a tragedy.

Our stories do not need to end this way.

Perhaps we can all learn to say, "I understand" and the smell of the roses will remind us that understanding is all that matters.

(R)evolutionary Love

I have had this title on my white board for a long time. I was not sure if it was a short or a much longer article. This version made its way on paper at this point in time. I still think there may be another longer version in the future.

Posted: 08/31/2015

Every moment is a fork in the road.
The road you take will shape your future.
Choose love over fear.

– Unknown Source

You may know that I spent some of the last six years teaching and facilitating Driver Alcohol Education classes for first offender drunk drivers. I always liked teaching the week 13 class the best. I started with the question:

Is stress good or bad?

Some answered yes, some no, while others wanted to know if it was a trick question. All of those responses were valid. The truth is, stress is good up to a point. It improves performance, but as we all know, too much stress will have the opposite effect. This is shown in the graphic below.

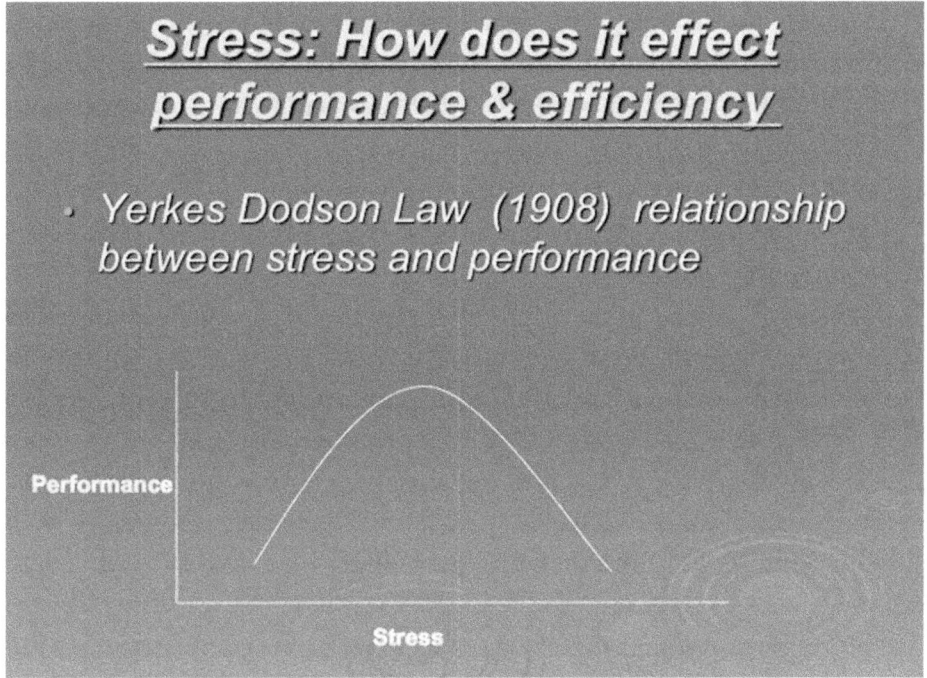

Stress and performance.

The obvious question comes up: Why is this so? As I try to explain, it will lead me into what I really want to share with you this week; something I believe can change the way you live your life, something that is about your very own survival.

As I have grown, and learned to accept change within the outside world, and myself, my thoughts on the meaning of survival have also changed or what you may say "evolved." Ever since 1859, when Charles Darwin published *On the Origin of Species by Means of Natural Selection, or the Preservation of Favored Races in the Struggle for Life*, we have learned that the survival of species is dependent on how well a species adapts, or evolves to handle all the threats to life that are constantly present in their environment.

It makes no difference to me whether you believe evolutionary or creationist theories as how the universe works. What I have come to learn is that the function of *stress*—the beauty and the rush of adrenaline, and cortisol running through our bodies—is to prepare us for survival from perceived threats in our environment. I am sure we all know that the immediate stress response is *fight or flight* which has only one purpose—survival.

However, I began to question what survival of the species meant to me as an individual. What did survival mean to me, when I spent so much of my life on *high alert* and hiding my truth? I was never very far from a stress response and ready to fight (verbally for me) or run away from people, dare they ever find out that I was not what I appeared to be. The levels of stress I was feeling internally for decades was ever so slowly taking its toll first, on being in relationships, and second, learning how to truly enjoy my life.

I could not understand why the survival of the species required me to hide, to be on constant alert, and why this was useful to me as an individual.

In 2007, I read an incredible book that was published in 2001: *A General Theory of Love* by T. Lewis, F. Amini, and R. Lannon that changed my world. They elegantly, eloquently, and clearly show how an individual's health and brain growth, in effect the individual's survival, is dependent on relationships and relatedness, and that as human beings the need to be in relationship with others is part of our physiological evolution. Our emotions, our feelings, our connections with others, and our need to be and live who we really are, are all part of our survival needs. In effect, they teach that love has a physiological basis for survival.

Some of us know how good it feels to be held, to be touched, to be cuddled. I am not talking about the culmination of intercourse and orgasm here, but rather that gentle and loving bonding brought by that other hormone—oxytocin, that does its work slowly and without the rush of adrenaline. It was a pleasant surprise that slow and long last-ing love is actually required for survival.

I started to look at survival in a different way. Stress is needed for the clear and present dangers, but love is needed for long-term growth and survival. That revelation was a kind of a head-slapping moment for me. The revolutionary idea that I could live my life operating from a place of love more than from a place of stress all the time, began to change my life. Perhaps living my truth was the best way for me to survive! In a sense, over the past eight years I have become a revolu-tionary and changed the most basic way I live my life.

– ☼ –

As a transgender woman who hid my truth for over 50 years, I well know what it is like to choose the path of fear believing that was my only path for survival. I am lucky that choosing to live in my true gender was not my only transition. I have learned to choose the path of love at every fork in the road I face.

Transitions come in many flavors. Some transitions may be simple, and we think of them as an organic change or simple evolution. Some-times we are not even aware of these transitions. However, many tran-sitions occur because we see them as our only path for survival. The path of fear will drive us to fight or flight or freeze. I have learned that there is always another path to survival and that is the path of love; loving yourself first, and then everyone else. For many this concept is revolutionary. To me, *(R)evolutionary Love* was my choice for survival.

I offer it for your consideration; it might work for you too!

Assimilation?

I had no idea that I was going in for this intensive of a procedure. I thought it would be just a little scraping on the surface of my skin. I was even more surprised to find out I was not prepared for the impact of this surgery afterwards.

Posted: 09/11/2015

I have had an internal debate about posting this. Like my book title, I evolved from "no" to "maybe" to "yes."

Last week, I had what I refer to as a few skin carvings. One was to remove a basal cell carcinoma on my forehead and the other to remove a benign mole on my breast.

I did not expect the latter to be fairly invasive as the doctor wanted to be sure there was enough "margin," so some digging was required. This was a week ago today, and in the picture below, I am showing the area of incision and what will end up as a lovely scar that is just below my bikini top. (Yes, I have been to the pool this week.)

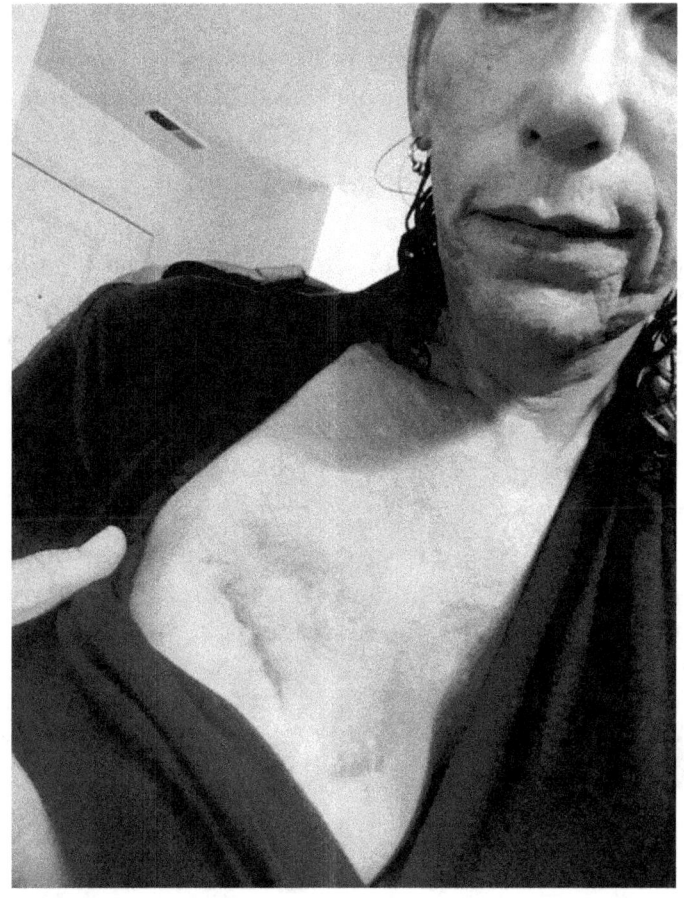

Marked.

However, I find it interesting as I am working with my parts that my three-year-old breasts—which feel like they have always been there and are a part of me—have now been "marked" by the same things that GGs (genetic girls) have when the have lumpectomies or breast cancer.

My transgender journey for over 50 years, dreaming of living in the body that would match how I knew myself, never had the thoughts that were now running through my mind! One part tells me it is another symbol of assimilation into womanhood, while another says it is something very different... yet that part would not be clear what it meant...

I have total clarity that my sense of self is that I am both a woman and a trans woman. I am comfortable holding these two ideas in parallel without any criticism or battling between them. I realize not everyone who transitions feels the same way. If you have read anything I have written before, you will know that I believe that it's OK with me too. Just the idea that I am thinking about the impact to me of this *invasive* surgery on my breast area makes me feel that I am living my true life and need to deal with things that many women have to deal with. This does not make it right or wrong, but it's a surprising observation on my experience. Everything is fine, and I am now on a healing journey.

Perhaps this is more of my journey of assimilation and brings me more in common with other women. Just perhaps...I would not change a thing. No matter what happens I know how blessed I have been.

Just thought I would share this. Thanks for listening.

Playing with House Money

It was hard trying to figure out my own value system. Not much came from my parents while growing up. I struggled with my inner secrets even through a 25-yearlong marriage and raising kids. This is another story that I knew I wanted to write, and as usual was never quite sure where it would go, and if there was a lesson in it or just a form of personal release.

Posted: 09/15/2015

We are not human beings having a spiritual experience.
We are spiritual beings having a human experience.

– Pierre Teilhard de Chardin

My father was born in the Bronx in 1914. By birthright, he was a U.S. citizen. His parents were immigrants from—as far as I know—somewhere in Eastern Europe. I never knew for sure where they came from, and I never knew them.

My father's mother died during the 1918 flu epidemic. I have only been able to piece together the bits and pieces of the stories. I find it hard to comprehend what it was like for him and his brothers to grow up in the 1920s and 1930s on the streets of New York in a broken/blended immigrant family. He never finished high school, and it seems he led an interesting life of survival on the streets. His birth name was Hyman Rabinowitz (which is what I knew him by), but I know during the war years he was known as Joe Gorrell—not wanting to be identified as Jewish. However, everyone just called him Blackie. I heard one story, that in his teens on the streets of the Bronx, he was known as little Blackie, as there was another with that name. Before World War II, he drove a junk truck from the East Coast through the Midwest and back. However, if there was one word that defined him, and his spirit, he was a gambler.

Blackie, and a very early version of me, late 1940s.

By the time I was a young boy, my consciousness knew that my parents argued about his gambling. I never longed for anything, but the reality was we did not have very much, as my parents and I lived in a two-room apartment in a large building in Brooklyn. Each morning he would walk to the paper stand and get the scratch sheet and the Morning Telegraph, so that he could handicap the day's horse races. I always listened to him on the phone as he called his bookie without having a clue what it was all about. My father worked six days a week in a gas station and often drove an AAA tow truck in the fifties. I remember one Wednesday when I was in the third grade when he let me stay home from school and took me with him to Belmont Park to watch the horse races. At first I was excited, although the other kids went to baseball games, I was going to the track! In the second race he asked me to pick a horse. I did, it won, and I was excited. The next race I picked again and it lost. I hated this. I realized it made me a sore loser, and I did not want to bet again. As I watched my father, losing never stopped him. It took me years to figure this out.

> **addiction**
>
> A compulsive behavior with something external to ourselves, and continuing that behavior in spite of the consequences to ourselves and others.

My father was a gambling addict. It did not matter if he won or lost. He needed the action of the event. Whether it was losing money he had or money he did not have, never mattered, he needed, he required the action to survive. However it developed, and I look at this without judgment, gambling was his spirit. From his own eyes, from his own heart, gambling defined Blackie.

Perhaps the apple did not fall too far from the tree. I never thought of myself as a gambler. Losing always felt worse that the excitement of winning to me. I never thought that I had any addictions. Convenient denial, perhaps? After a few years of teaching and counseling in a substance abuse clinic and using the definition of addiction above, I finally had to admit that I apparently had a compulsive behavior that was....what was it...defining, acting out or hiding...my true spirit. I cross-dressed—I could not stop—I could not control it! Was this so different than my father's gambling? I know that defined him, but what in the world defined me? What was and is my true spirit? Why would I hide so much of myself? What was I afraid of?

I hated losing! If I ever dared to let my true spirit out, I feared the losing, the losses of everything and everyone in my life. This fear blocked me at all turns. Until the moment I could admit my truth to myself and accept it. I still feared the loss but there was a glimmer of hope that I could also possibly win something here. After the decades of hiding, denying and avoiding my true spirit, I chose to move forward and go on the journey to live my truth.

It is now over five years since I made the choice that allowed me to win my life back. It is over four years since I have been living as the woman I truly am. My relationship with my father—who has been gone for over 20 years has changed and is still changing—all for the better. I think I can understand him more and accept him more.

Sometimes, in my dreams, I let him know this. He lets me know he loves me—which is something he never said when he was here. My relationship with myself is also changing and also for the better, and I remind myself each and every day.

For those who have ever gone to a casino and won, and then continue to gamble with those winnings, there is a saying that you are "playing with house money." You can enjoy the action without worrying about losing your own money. Once I claimed and chose to live as my true spirit, and as myself, I have found that I have won so much of myself, my spirit, that I am playing out the rest of my life with house money. But is has nothing to do with finances.

No Bang, No Whimper, Just a Small Smile

This is a story of my personal evolution. I am both a student and a teacher of change and the fact that we are changing in each moment. However, even I am surprised by some of my own changes as I learn who I am in each moment.

Posted: 09/22/2015

*The curious paradox is that when I accept myself
just as I am, then I can change*

– Carl Rogers, On Becoming a Person

I think it occurred during sometime during the summer, but honestly I cannot be sure.

It wasn't something that I thought about very much. Now that I think about it, it was more like a thought that used to be in my dreams, but never a goal that I was actively pursuing.

I transitioned four years ago, and never ever had a thought of hiding the fact I am transgender. Gosh, I have written a book, been interviewed in various media outlets and now write these blogs that announce "My Transgender Life" for the world to read. My logic has been that I hid who I was for almost 60 years. I have no intention of spending any more time hiding who I am or any energy on rewriting my personal history of who I used to be.

With this logic, as part of my core sense of myself, I wrote a few weeks ago that I could hold both the fact that I am a transgender woman and a woman in a comfortable balance. Also having a public identity as being transgender, I felt that part of introducing myself to new people would include the fact that I was transgender, and possibly use this as a teaching moment. Perhaps there is a part of me that has believed that the best defense is a good offense, so I would generally put this fact out fairly early in meeting new people.

I did not even realize when this all changed.

Somewhere deep inside me there was a shift of my internal tectonic plates as my frame of reference of how I saw myself changed. The shift occurred so deeply inside of me I never noticed it even though its impact was great.

Perhaps it was due to external forces. There was certainly the earthquake of the entire Jenner story back in April. Perhaps it was due to being interviewed on what my thoughts were about the story. Perhaps it was the appearance of so many transgender TV reality shows.

Or perhaps it was the realization and self-acceptance this summer that I was OK after swimming or showering to just let my hair air dry, without needing to have it look straight and perfect in order to face the world each day. Perhaps it is just the right time, as I am now four years post-transition, and this kind of change is a pretty standard step on these types of journeys.

I suspect I will not really know the reasons but the change did happen.

It seems that I am now able to interact with a variety of people with absolutely no mention that I am trans. My identity has not changed—at least I do not think so—but my internal frame of reference definitely has. Although some people question my bio when I state I am a father of three, when I look in a mirror, I see a woman looking back at me and have difficulty remembering the man I used to be. I know who I was, I own that part of my journey, and I hope that I will never deny anything that is part of my story. However, in these present moments when just meeting and chatting with strangers, or new acquaintances, I no longer feel defensive or feel the need to be the one to introduce the fact that I am trans. They may question, they may suspect, they may even know, but I have crossed an internal and even an external threshold that this information is no longer important in defining me.

I am aware this has created a new paradox for me. I write describing my various journeys as a transgender person, yet I am starting to live as if this is not that big of a deal. For awhile this was making my head spin, but I am beginning to understand what Carl Rogers means by the curious paradox, and each day I am becoming more and more OK with this.

I interact with people in stores, at the town pool, and even my women friends and colleagues who know that I am trans, some of whom even knew me before I transitioned that tell me they do not see a trans woman, they just see and think of me as a woman, and interact with me as a close and supportive friend. It has taken me a while to let this sink in, but I think it has. It seems it has taken me longer to reach this point than many of them. Curious indeed!

This is the way the world ends
Not with a bang but a whimper.

– T. S. Eliot

For many trans people the act of transition is the culmination of an internal battle that represents the end of a world that they felt they did not belong in. Some can do this quietly, but for most there is a large BANG, as it impacts so many people around them. However, that battle is never the end of the internal war. If you have not experienced this battle and are not trans, you may not understand that the war is not over.

Your old world may or may not end, although your new world may well be beginning. Your new world of self-discovery, self-understanding, and self-acceptance can take you on roads and adventures never dreamed of. There is no specific time period or map for this journey

I did not even notice when one of my worlds ended. There was no bang, no whimper, just a small smile forming on my face.

You too may even find, curiously as it may be, that you are not even aware of how you are changing as day by day you are just living your true life. Enjoy the journey!

Bad Dreams

I had no plans for this one. It was totally spontaneous. This is where I have learned to trust the process and go with the flow. I hope there is a lesson here for others too.

Posted: 09/28/2015

I've had bad dreams too many times
To think that they don't mean much anymore
Fine times have gone and left my sad home
Friends who once cared just walk out my door

– Eric Kaz, Libby Titus, "Love Has No Pride"

I woke up early Sunday morning after I had a bad dream. It wasn't quite a nightmare. Those are the ones where I wake up just at the point where the monster is about to swallow me whole, or the car I'm in goes off a road on a high mountain and is tumbling and tumbling as I wake with a start!

The nightmare.

This was one of those dreams that are just so unsettling as they unfold in your consciousness. You may know the feeling. You are both an observer of the action, which by some strange sense of time you already know what is going to happen, yet you cannot do anything about it, and are also an actor in it and are performing the required role of being you!

You know there is lesson you're supposed to learn, but as soon as you wake, the entire dream starts to slip away from your mind, and is often hard to recapture. Sometimes this is a good thing, but sometimes there is a strange feeling that you carry through the day and are not sure why. This was one of those times.

— ☼ —

Let me set the scene.

I was watching an ex-partner on the phone talking to the "authorities," and telling them I failed to replace the bald tires on our car. As she hung up the phone, she noticed me watching her. She came over with quite the smug look on her face and announced that they would be soon coming to take me away and it is over.

I wanted to question what in the world she was talking about, but it seems that in these dreams I never, ever have a speaking part. Then the scene repeated time after time after time. Like one of those sports highlight films that are shown over and over, before I managed to pull myself awake.

It made no sense to me while it was happening, or when I awoke, and it was a bit frightening.

— ☼ —

There are different ways one can look at dreams. I subscribe to the idea that dreams are to both teach you a lesson and allow you to practice for some future event or challenge. So, what am I to make of this one, as a few parts of me just want to run away from it as fast as they can?

But, as I think about particular dream, its meaning seems to be coming to me, and I was surprised that this is actually an old story of mine that I did not recognize, and perhaps may be in process of playing out again in some new way. It is my story of self-acceptance that I am transgender and knew that I had to do something about it.

Here is my dream interpretation:

The ex-partner was not another person, but rather it was me, this present version of me, living my true life, while the "I" in the dream was the old "male" version of me letting his tread run bare and refusing to replace the old tires as he was so tired of traveling that road over and over, but refused to take any action on moving forward in any direction. Someone had to force the issue, so this present version of me called the "authorities." All so that I could/would at last learn to love myself and live my truth.

Now, this sounds familiar and correct, but there are still so many unanswered questions.

Why am I having this dream?

I know that there is no issue with living as my true gender, but is there something else that I need to prepare for?

Am I refusing to take another step into some other unknown?

What is this is asking me to practice for?

I sense there is something else out there. Part of me is afraid and part of me wants the adventure. I know there will be change. After all, change is the only constant in this world, and I do not want to ever let my tires get bald again. I hope there will not be losses but it took me 60 years to learn to not let that fear get in the way. Right? Right!

I do need to think about this. My interpretation sure makes sense to me, and maybe that dream was not as bad as I thought. It is always a matter of perspective. I still need to figure out what I need to practice, but it is no longer frightening.

Maybe even the bad dreams have something good to say!

Optical and Other Illusions

For many people who transition genders, we feel we have no choice to live our lives as how we see ourselves in our mind's eye. I find it interesting to get past myself and learn how others have seen me both pre and post-transition. Sometimes this is illuminating.

Posted: 10/04/2015

Over the years I have been fascinated by my relationship with mirrors and how it has changed.

There were the years when I truly hated what I saw when I looked in the mirror. I hated that I had to wear glasses to see anything at all; I hated seeing my uncontrollable wavy and curly hair; and yes, as you know by now, I was so confused to see that boy, then man, looking back at me when I sensed that there was something terribly wrong.

There were the years after college when I lived on my own, and had long hair, and morphed from the hippie look of embroidered jeans, to the glam days of platform shoes before I got married. The mirror was my friend in those days. The illusion I saw of someone different than who I really was, was more pleasing to me, but it still did not soothe my soul.

The years when I was married and raised a family, I had so many mixed episodes with mirrors and the illusions I saw back. There were the good days, the great days of being Dad, when nothing else in the world mattered at all—not the future, not my career, not my underlying dysphoria. There were days when there was the feeling of being trapped, and I wondered whether happiness for me was an illusion that would never see the light of day. I never was quite sure who I would see back in the mirror each morning, and how hard it would be to get through each day.

I kept going. Day after day, year after year. Some days were plodding, while some were filled with adventure and excitement, but I usually felt I was at the mercy of forces that were outside of my control.

– ☼ –

I was taught that what I saw in the mirror was a view of reality. It took me a long time to understand that the mirror was only a two-dimensional representation—one with no depth at all, of me—a real multidimensional person. It was only an *illusion* of who I was. Yet, this illusion had so much power that I never knew it was not the true me.

– ☼ –

The power of illusion fought to take over my life after my marriage ended. In 2001, I was single again at 54 years old and after 25 years of marriage, after raising a fabulous family. My apartment became a huge "closet" for me as my gender dysphoria was allowed to run wild. I was a closeted cross-dresser (or so I thought at the time) and would never leave the safety of my apartment. After work, I spent almost every evening staring at the "woman" in the mirror, changing my outfits uncountable times.

Were the optical illusions I saw reflected really me? I wanted this to be true, oh I wanted it so much, but was so confused, so afraid and so full of shame. I knew these feeling were not illusions. I took picture after picture in the mirror to prove her existence. I would look at the pictures over and over to prove her existence. A battle was raging within me as to whether the male version or female version of me was the reality or the illusion. As I have mentioned before, deep down I always knew the answer, but the confusion, fear, and shame would not let that answer bubble to the surface for many more years.

When and after I transitioned, I learned that there are so many more illusions besides what we see in the mirror. In my book, *No Maybe? Yes! Living My Truth* I share an interview with my youngest son and his wife, when I asked him if he had any losses when I transitioned. Their reply on illusions is, I believe, priceless. Here is an excerpt of the conversation:

Grace: I have a question here that asks, do you think my transition has cost you any losses? Are there other things beside the awkwardness you mentioned earlier?

Elie: Well, there was not a loss here. I was worried that Grace would be so vastly different from Larnie that there would be a loss, but I don't feel that you are that different.

Grace: Interesting, because I feel I am vastly different. Since I no longer am hiding who I truly am, I think I am more open and softer. I think I live in a space of compassion now, to others.

Becca: Elie has said that the masculine/feminine piece has never been an issue for you, (to Elie) but since you always want to remember the good things, and not the bad, the biggest thing you lost was the illusion that your dad was happy for his whole life, before he transitioned. The thing that you thought was that everything was always good, always. What you lost was the illusion that things were always good, always. That was really hard for you: to realize that your dad really did not have a happy life.

Elie: Yeah, We always had the coolest family on the block and always had people over. I had good friends whom you knew who never let me over at their house because they had a weird family situation or a weird home or whatever... and maybe we had a similar situation, but we always had an open door.

Elie: It seemed like you were just living your life the way you were supposed to. I see this all the time. Like people are 28 and say, I got a job, I got married, I have kids; that's just what I do. This is just what you do. So many people seem to do that. We really don't want to live like that. That's wrong, that must have sucked.

Becca: (to Elie) That's the biggest thing that happened after we found out your dad was transgender. You said, "I need my life not to be living like that. My dad has apparently been unhappy for 60 years; we need to make sure we don't do that." We always make sure we are living the life we want to live.

Grace: And that's become my mission, when I heard you say this.

Becca: It sounds so terrifying to not live the life you want. It is so sad.

I am good with mirrors now, and yes my kids understood and understand. Not living your true life is so sad. I learned that it is never too late to live your truth. Be True!

Choices

Let's just be clear. Being trans is not a choice. Those who believe differently are just plain wrong! This is so hard to accept for those of us who are as well for the many who are not. Our struggle is not in being who we are, but is about what we do about it and the fear of losing those in our life.

Posted: 10/12/2015

Life is full of choices!

Sometimes I struggle to decide whether I think this is a cliché or just a fact of life. I know that there are certain facts that are not choices. I believe that knowing our identity as one of them. I do subscribe to the following:

> *We do not have a choice in being transgender.*
> *We do have a choice in what we do about it.*

Whenever I think about all the choices I have made in my life—getting married, having kids, and ultimately transitioning—I always wrestled with the choices in front of me. Which path should I take? What are the pros; the cons? Am I being selfish? Will someone get hurt? So many voices inside of me are arguing for each position it is often hard to be living in my own head! I constantly wondered why in the world are they doing that?

There have been so many times I have been faced with life-changing choices. None of them were easy; as I let all those inner voices have their say. For most of those choices, I sat without any movement for a long, long time before I took any action at all.

I suspect that almost everyone has seen the movie *The Matrix*. I marveled at how quickly Neo chose the Red Pill (rather than the blue one) in the classic scene and was willing to go down the rabbit hole. It took me over five decades to be willing to go down my own rabbit hole to chase my truth!

– ☼ –

After my marriage ended in 2001, I was again single and wrestled with so many choices about my life. Deep down inside I knew that I was transgender but not another soul in the world knew of my inner struggle. My body and brain were still waging the same war they had- for decade upon decade. My body had needs! You know what I mean. I got horny; I got turned on by women or thoughts of women. I needed release; pleasure it is called. I needed to reach that rolling alignment of neurons firing in unison as it travelled through my body and culminated in that release all of which we call orgasm. My body needed it, demanded it! Then there were parts of my mind that took over with the pangs of guilt and telling me it was so wrong as I was not really a man!

It did not matter whether I was with a partner or by myself, my body demanded that its needs were fulfilled. I was in my mid-fifties and finding it harder and harder to give the body what it wanted as it was struggling to get the release it desired.

Every night after work, my apartment was my big closet where the man disappeared and the woman appeared and dreamt that someday she would be real. It was her version of Pinocchio, as she wanted to be a "real girl!"

The war continued; my body wanted sex and pleasure, my mind wanted to live her truth. Like Neo in *The Matrix* I had to choose between pills, although they were both blue ones. One pill would allow the body to get what it desired, or as Neo was offered, to wake up in my bed and believe whatever I wanted to believe.

Viagra, for the body.

Viagra, the choice for the body

The other pill, would undoubtedly allow me to stay in Wonderland and take me down the rabbit hole deeper and deeper with no way to return.

Estradiol, 2MG. The choice for the mind.

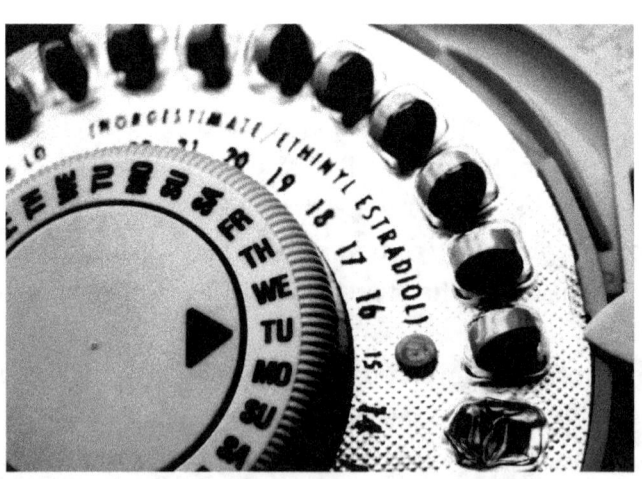

Estradiol, the choice for the mind.

There was never a voice like Morpheus within me to tell me it was my last chance to choose. I knew that the first choice was the easy one, yet even when I chose it, the inner battle continued. The voices in my head to choose the rabbit hole were getting louder and stronger, even though the voices expressing fear and uncertainty were just as loud. In January 2010, I chose to go down the rabbit hole and find my truth.

I have made many choices in my life. Some turned out well and some were less successful. One choice in my life was to seek and follow my truth. It really does matter that it took me so many years before I did. I never look back; I never ask that useless "what if" question. The fact that I always knew my truth but spent so much of my life denying it and letting my body have its needs fulfilled and listen to the voices of fear and shame are all in the past. I am happy to share them now because I know that although my own specific journey is unique, there are many others on journeys with variations on this theme and it is so hard to talk about our internal wars between our bodies and our minds when we are transgender.

For me, the trip down the rabbit hole is one that I am so happy to be taking as I go deeper and deeper into my truth. My body and mind are both at peace as they travel as partners along my adventures in my own Wonderland of just discovering and being me in each moment.

I have chatted with many friends about how challenging these choices are as all the voices in their heads argue endlessly and get stuck. I have been there and know what that feels like, and I never can tell anyone how to choose his or her path. My own experience has allowed me to reflect that my body never knew or cared about my mind's truth, but over time, my mind's dreams have outlasted my body's perceived needs. This is just my story, and may not be true for anyone else. I can only repeat what Morpheus told Neo:

All I can offer is the Truth. Nothing More.

If you seek yours, it will be yours and yours only!

– ☼ –

A big thank you to Lana W for helping create the world of *The Matrix* and teaching us all about these choices.

Postscript, June 2016: *Since I wrote this, now Lily W has also transitioned to live her true life. It just feels right to extend my thanks to both sisters for what they created and how they make a difference in the world.*

Grandma's Closet

It is hard for me to pick favorites here. However, I love the chance I had to drop in these old pictures. Honestly, I cannot stop looking at the picture of my mom as a younger woman. This is sadly not how I have remembered her. I can't explain how or why, but writing this has brought me closer to both her and my father even though they are long gone.

Posted: 10/19/2015

It was the early 1950s. I was around five or six years old. You may remember those days when life was pretty simple. My parents and I lived in a two-room apartment in a large building in the middle of the Flatbush area in Brooklyn. I had no idea what we had or didn't have in comparison to others. Even back then we had a 13-inch Dumont television, and I spent most of my time plastered in front of it, watching Roy Rogers, Gene Autry and Hopalong Cassidy. My father even had a 1947 Dodge that got us around. Of course, it was black, as all cars seemed to be back then.

My Saturday mornings were a treat of cartoons and fairy tales as I sat as close to the tube as I could watching Crusader Rabbit, Lamb Chop and Charley Horse. There was also Winky Dink, and I could not wait to stick that plastic screen on the front of the picture tube and use the different color crayons to find the message and path to safety.

None of these Saturday morning adventures compared to my Sundays. This was family day! I mean *family day*! My mom, dad and me—

and my aunts, uncles and cousins would spend the day at Grandma's. Way back then, it was always a special day. That was so very long ago!

My memories of getting in the car and driving to another section of Brooklyn were a grand adventure. Back then the size of my accessible world was measured in city blocks, and each neighborhood was full of wonder. I still had no idea how big and strange the world was.

My grandma on the stoop in front of her apartment.

We were going to the Brownsville section of Brooklyn. This is where my parents grew up and Grandma still lived. She was the only grandparent I ever knew and even then when she was apparently in her fifties, she was already an old woman who had lived a hard life. However, at the time, I had no idea...she was just Grandma who had chicken soup with matzo balls! That alone was worth the trip! My mom was the second of seven children and they were all there on Sundays. It was always a full house. Crazy and fun at the same time.

My mom.

Grandma lived in a row of old tenement buildings in Brownsville. She lived on the third floor. Her apartment had two bedrooms, a living room, and a big kitchen with a cast iron coal stove in it. This is how the apartment was heated and how meals were cooked. There was always coal burning there all year long. There was a coal bin in the basement, and I always thought it was fun to help my dad and my uncles tie a pail to the rope and pulley and haul the pails full of coal from the basement to the third floor through the center staircase. The apartment always smelled from coal gas, and although I loved being there, I was glad when I left. I did not understand why, way back then. I was so young and this is just how it was.

– ☼ –

Each Sunday trip to Grandma's—I never even knew she had another name—was something I loved. It was expected and it was comforting. To this day, I still do not know why I feel this way. It was so different back then…

My dad and me.

However, there were the very special days that happened every now and then. Most of my cousins were a few years older than me, and sometimes they would spontaneously announce it is going to be "Showtime!" We would all head into Grandma's bedroom and go through her closet and find some clothes so that we put on a show for all the adults.

That closet was amazing! She still had grandpa's clothes. He had died before I was born. I am pretty sure the piles of clothes represented my grandma's generation. Immigrants, who came here with nothing, had large families and survived through the years of depression and world war. No wonder this woman in her fifties was already an old lady.

There were so many things to choose from. Sometimes I grabbed the old men's suits and long jackets. Sometimes I grabbed some of Grandma's dresses and wool coats. For some reason, this felt better to me. Back then I had no conscious experience of what my truth was, and how I hid it. None of cousins cared as we were all just dressing up and having fun. Looking back, yes, those were simpler times. So much simpler, indeed! Just the joys of a childhood experience without a care in the world. The boomer generation was much different than that of my parents or grandparents. Even with the challenges in my life, I cannot even imagine what they lived through.

Grandma's closet was the first place I got to dress up in women's clothes. By the time I was eight, I was already sneaking into my mom's closet to try on her dresses. This was no longer "Showtime" for the adults. This was secretive and shameful. This was my truth trying to find a way out of hiding. It was scary, and I was all alone.

The days got more difficult until my truth self-found her way out in my sixties. The journey itself was hard. Not only for me but also for all those in my life. Now there is no more hiding, no more questioning. It has been a long journey since those simpler days in Grandma's closet.

It may sound a little strange, but life is simpler once again.

Everyday Transitions

The theme of change has come forward to me once again. Everyone changes; everyone transitions; all the time!

Posted: 10/26/2015

I remember when my kids where young. We had a measuring chart on the wall where each year we marked how much they had grown.

Growing was exciting for both the kids and for me and my ex—the parents. We also had another ritual each year around the Jewish New Year when we would take some time and write down what we learned and what we were thankful for the past year. We often marveled at the changes in us individually and as a family over the past year.

I don't quite remember when all this stopped!

In 2001 when my marriage ended, my youngest turned 18 and was getting ready to go off to college. One of my children was still in college and one was finished. It is still not clear to me whether it changed before or after this point. I myself was pretty consumed with all the changes and transitions in my own life, and looking back now, all I can see is a cloud of confusion. No matter how hard I try to look back at this period, clarity continues to escape me. It is hard for me to admit this!

Moving out...the end of a 25 year marriage...the push/pull of my buried dysphoria were all creating an internal storm of change in me that now, looking back, can explain my lack of clarity, that at last I can seem to own without a need to blame or deny.

I have come to understand that the journey to reach this point is just another everyday transition that occurs all throughout our lives. More important, I understand if I do not learn to accept these every-day transitions, it will always cloud my thinking and make me crazy!

– ☼ –

In 2008, I took the risk to come out of my self-imposed shell and take my first baby steps into the transgender community. It did not take me long to learn that the commonly used word, transition, be-came a much bigger and somewhat magical word—transition! When I heard that word spoken, when I saw it written, it seemed that my brain could not wrap around any other references for this word and it would only draw pictures in my brain of changing gender. As I met others, I asked if they transitioned, will they transition, do they want to transition. The answers were as varied as the people I asked.

If I heard the word used in any context other than "gender transi-tion," my brain seemed to go on red alert, and the internal sirens were blaring, and the anxiety of fear and shame was wondering how they might know what I was considering internally. Sometimes it was hard to slow down my heartrate as the adrenaline was pumping though me as fast as it could. Warning! Danger! Get ready to run! I was not even sure myself, but fear, confusion, and shame were still associated with that word from 2008 to 2010 when I knew I was definitely on that path.

. – ☼ –

I have been sharing my story with you for some time now, both through my book and these blogs. It amazes me what comes up for me each week—what I learn about myself that I have not even thought about…and even more so, my willingness to share it all with you. It no longer generates fear or confusion or even shame. I have learned that there is no magic to transition, but it is an everyday occurrence. Cer-tainly some changes, some transitions have larger impacts on our lives, but I have learned that each and every transition is important in itself.

Some transitions are forced upon us. Some may come from deep inside, either spontaneously or through a journey of internal wrestling. This work is not often seen from outside, and we can struggle to let others know of these experiences. I think we often need to let others know of these battles to confirm ourselves in some manner. Telling our stories is a way we do this, and can often help others with their own journeys.

There is a bottom line here. Change and transition occur every day and for everyone. In some way it can be special and ordinary at the same time. It depends on knowing that it is true, and how easily we can first accept the fact, and then accept the occurrence. For those of us who have transitioned our gender as we live in the world, it can often consume so much of our life and being. Now that some time has passed for me—it has been four years—I have reached a place where I can honor it as part of my personal history, and look forward to the next transition in my life, and the adventure of discovering what it may be.

Perhaps I should hang a new growth chart on my wall so that I can mark each of my new everyday transitions!

– ☼ –

In my book I wrote what I have learned about change and transitions:

> So far I have learned that I am changing each moment, each and every day. I am not the same person I was yesterday or who I will become tomorrow. I have learned to be excited by this and now look forward to it. My old parts that felt they had to control everything so tightly are relieved because they were fighting against this belief. Change is constant. Change is inevitable.

I'll leave a question for you…

Who are you now?

…and now?

…and now?

The Circus

This is another spontaneous unplanned article. I love when these interactions become the basis of what I write about. The observation is about the different roles we play in our lives just trying to figure out who we are and how to make it through each day the best we can.

Posted: 11/02/2015

Each Tuesday night we have an open house at The Tiffany Club of New England (TCNE). For well over 30 years the club has been an open and safe support group welcoming members and newcomers who seek support in exploring, expressing, or questioning their feelings of gender variance. The club may well be unique in that it has a brick-and-mortar facility that is open year round. The club itself is a 501(c)(3) registered charity that has evolved over its lifetime as people come and go according to their own journeys, which I am quick to point out are always unique. I encourage people to share their own stories and journeys, but try to refrain from telling others how to travel their own unique paths. I think this is good advice for all of us, whether trans or not, in all our relationships. Sometimes I joke about this as "Grace's Rule" — as I advise newcomers with:

> *When someone tells you what you should do, run as fast and as far as you can. Listen to each person's story and then after careful thought, write you own story and choose your own path.*

TCNE has been such an important part of my own journey (which I share in my book), that I have found that the present path I am on includes getting to the club on most Tuesdays to give back and provide support to others just as support was provided to me when I was in need of it. Since every person's journey is so unique, mine included, sometimes I am able to provide support for others and sometimes I will say the wrong thing at the wrong time, and not provide the support I hoped to. I have learned to own my mistakes and will apologize—which in itself has been a challenging lesson for me. I have learned that these are lessons about all relationships; sometimes we do not seem to know where the words that have come out of us originated, and what their impact on others may be. Good intention or bad intention, sometimes it just comes out wrong! I have learned to be gentle with and to myself, and now know that every moment has an opportunity to learn something new about myself.

– ☼ –

Over the past few months, the Tuesday night open house has had great attendance with anywhere from 10 to 15 people often showing up. We advertise that we are open from 7:00 to 9:00 p.m., but often times a good size group hangs in the living room for various deep and personal discussions and support on their journeys, for a few more hours.

This past Tuesday was no exception. To borrow a term from Billy Joel's *Piano Man*, by around 7:30 p.m., "the regular crowd shuffled in" and there was at least one first timer, who was nervous and excited at the same time; desperately seeking support and most probably wondering what universe they just walked into. Many voices telling their stories, once again, and asking questions of the newcomer, and of course, offering advice from their own viewpoint. We are all human and that is just the way it is, right!

Later in the evening, there was a good group getting into the deep. The sharing of weekly challenges and successes of each of their journeys. The offering of support and experiences that sometimes were hitting the mark and sometimes missing by a wide margin. The insight and the triggering were all part of the weekly conversations.

Sometimes I hear from others the next day in private conversation whether my comments hit the mark or not. I am happy to receive the feedback whether good or bad, as that is the only way I can learn. This past week I received both types of feedback, and that is not uncommon. I did apologize for what I could have done better. I did receive a note from one of the girls who was there that I want to share with you all. Pearl is relatively new to the club and early on her journey. She has just starting to take some writing classes, and I thought the note I received was so elegant and eloquent, and she has allowed me to share it here.

I thought your comment to Britney last night about how we are all on our own journeys...a good reminder. Of course, I feel my journey right now is pulled over at a comfortable rest stop with a scenic view. But I think what comes out is everyone's fragility in their journey. To change metaphors, anyone of us could be a circus to themselves. Magician (make things appear/disappear), juggler, tightrope walker, strongman, lion tamer (spouses), clown and, of course, the person who comes around after to clean up the mess that dropped. And for some, you could add being the person shot out of a cannon. Sounds strong, but we are still fragile. The reminder is we are lucky to have TCNE.

– Pearl

I think Pearl has summed it up about all our journeys and how important it is to be able to share these in a safe environment. Yes, I am pretty sure each of us is fragile no matter what façade we show to the world. It is often hard to admit this to not only others but to ourselves.

Sometimes we just need to sit and listen to others who have some of the same—but not all the same—types of experiences that we do. When we do, then I will go back to Billy Joel and think he also described some of the Tuesday night conversations at TCNE, as we share and support each other...

Sing us a song you're the piano man
Sing us a song tonight

Well we're all in the mood for a melody
And you got us feeling alright.

– Billy Joel "Piano Man"

What We Have Learned from Apollo 13

I thought I learned to stay away for the political issues. I guess this was not quite as true as I wanted it to be. I may have set a personal record on using quotes in this one.

Posted: 11/06/2015

Houston, we have a problem.

This has been another week, when the dark side of fear has conquered—for at least the moment—doing what is right and treating all people with respect and compassion, no matter how different they may be from you, even if you do not understand them.

> *Fear is the path to the dark side. Fear leads to anger.*
> *Anger leads to hate. Hate leads to suffering.*
>
> – Yoda

In Houston, earlier this week, Proposition 1, which would add protections for gender identity in the city's nondiscrimination ordinance, was defeated. In effect, the citizens of Houston threw the baby out with the bathwater, as they defeated the entire nondiscrimination bill since it added the words "gender identity" as a protected class. The opponents once again claimed it was the "bathroom bill" and were successful in creating enough fear in the citizens to be afraid of those of us who are transgender.

Yes, Houston, we have a problem!

— ☼ —

I have lived with fear for so much of my life. Being transgender, I lived in fear of being discovered, and the shame that would fall over and bury me. I hid so people would not know my truth. I hid it from myself for so long, which numbed me out from fully being and participating freely in the world. I know so many other trans people who have shared the same feelings with me. It has taken us so long to learn who we are and get to a point of self-acceptance. Many of us have, while many are still exploring their own paths of discovery.

Fear is also present in people who do not travel this path of gender variance.

Fear is a natural reaction to moving closer to the truth.

– Pema Chödrön

In order to come to terms with my true self, my true nature, my true sense of who I am, I had to learn about fear. I am far from a Jedi Master, but I understand that fear is the path to the dark side, and I no longer want to go there. This takes a conscious effort and work on my part. It has taken me so many years to learn, and still I get to learn it each day. This is so important to me that I open the first chapter of my book with the following quote:

What is needed, rather than running away or controlling or suppressing or any other resistance, is understanding fear; that means, watch it, learn about it, come directly into contact with it. We are to learn about fear, not how to escape from it.

– Jiddu Krishnamurti

– ☼ –

In the clip from Apollo 13, we see how fear can be conquered by teamwork, and a concerted effort by a team. In space and on Earth there was no doubt fear, yet every one stayed calm in order to solve the problem and return everyone to safety. I believe there is a lesson here. We cannot let fear beget fear. We all know where this leads, and know that it never solves anything.

We, who are transgender, have done nothing wrong. However, for many who do not understand our experience, it is easy, although sad, to walk down the path of fear. This past week, I was invited to train a group of high school teachers who had so many questions about how they can best deal with some of the students in the school who were exploring gender. I asked these teachers whether the student population had the same concerns and fears as the teachers were expressing to me, and they honestly shared that it was the teachers' concern to do the right thing, as for most of the student body, it was no big deal. Hearing the openness and honesty of the teachers, makes me glad to say that I will be working with them more to help them learn.

We can easily forgive a child who is afraid of the dark;
the real tragedy of life is when men are afraid of the light.

– Plato

Sometimes, I refuse to say the word "problem." I often will replace it with the word "opportunity." I am comfortable in my own skin and am happy to use each moment as a teaching moment. I also believe that for me each moment is a learning moment.

If we learn to open our hearts, anyone,
including the people who drive us crazy,
can be our teacher.

– Pema Chödrön

We will all be stronger together if we are willing to teach and learn from each other. It will not be easy, and I hope we choose the path where the light is.

People Like Us

This one is about diversity. I think of it as a teaching lesson. Yes, this is a pretty consistent theme that I have, as I often attempt to teach it through a different lens.

Posted: 11/12/2015

I like to talk about what I call "Grace's Paradox."

> *"We are all the same...each of us is unique"*

In the Preface of my book, No! Maybe? Yes! Living My Truth, I commented on this very fact...

> *Most of us either take this for granted or forget it. In our very human need to belong, to be taken care of, our brains are wired to sort through those who are like us and those who are different. We often unconsciously sort and categorize, and then our culture adds labels of good and bad to these groupings.*

I can't quite remember when I learned that there was a difference between people like us and people not like us. Growing up in Brooklyn, my neighborhood and elementary school seemed pretty much homogenous (not that I understood that word way back then). Most of my friends and neighbors were second-generation Jewish baby boomers, already well on the path to assimilation. I had no idea we were part of a diverse minority, even less so, a minority that suffered through the genocide of World War II. High school became more diverse, as did college and then, of course, crossing the threshold into the "real world" unveiled the differences, and the separation in everyday life.

Perhaps my first 21 years of life were pretty sheltered, as I did not understand the concept that I was seeing in the real world. I still don't really understand it.

> **Xenophobia** [zen-uh-foh-bee-uh, zee-nuh-]
>
> *noun,*
>
> 1. An unreasonable fear or hatred of foreigners or strangers or of that which is foreign or strange.
>
> Dictionary.com

Apparently we not only want to be with people like us, but we also seem afraid of those who are not like us. When I was young, I was taught that the United States and especially New York City was called the "melting pot." Miss Liberty welcomed all with the words, "Give me your tired, your poor, your huddled masses yearning to be free."

But, really, was this so? Do we melt together and become one society? Or do we continue to separate and be in fear of others? Where is the balance, and how do we become more integrated and better without the fear and the hatred?

— ☼ —

For the past few years, I taught about diversity and used the following chart. There are so many ways that we are different both as individuals, and as subcultures.

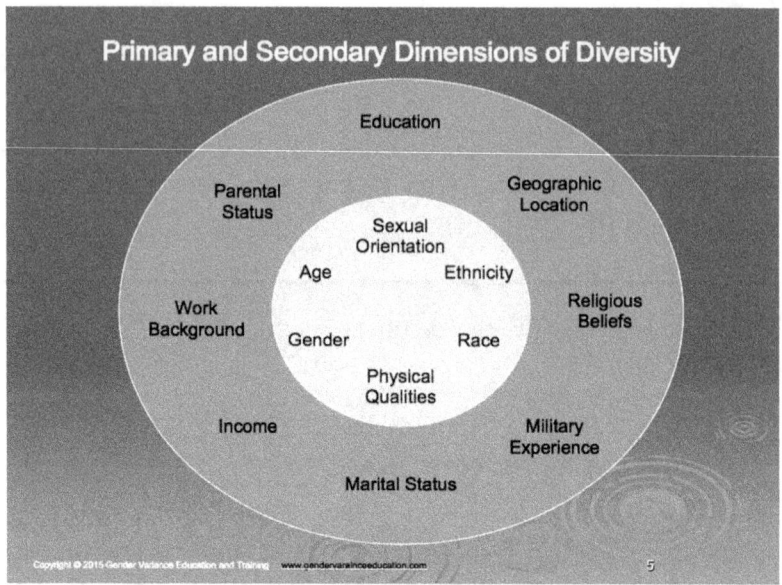

Primary and secondary diversity dimensions.

Whenever I show this slide, I ask the group why any single item is more important than the other. Although I would like an answer, I do not often receive one. The question seems to stump most people. I follow with an exploration of prejudice. I admit that I have prejudices and that I am sure that each person has them too. The question is really if we are ruled and controlled by them. Can we learn to question them and find their source? Are they our own beliefs or a cultural belief handed down to us from someone or somewhere else? Are we willing to learn, to listen, and to accept that our differences and uniqueness, is what makes life not only interesting and exciting but provides so much opportunity for growth?

I spent so much of my life hiding because I was different—being transgender. When I look at the chart above, this is only one single aspect of me and my own categories of diversity. Certainly I make a claim to the label, as I even title these blogs under "My Transgender Life." But this is only a single aspect of me, and one that I hope is not necessarily the most important. I dream that in a few years the idea that a person who is transgender will get the "ho hum" treatment from most people, as this may become the least interesting thing about them.

Remember I am just like you…I am unique as are you!

– ☼ –

I totally get that we want to be with people like us. I think we believe it is simpler, safer, and will perhaps lead to more understanding, acceptance, and love.

Seinfeld clip on YouTube.

I wonder how true this may be, and perhaps a clip from the *Seinfeld* episode, "Falling in Love with Someone Who's Just Like You" (https://www.youtube.com/watch?v=NVDT1ARABvE) may illustrate it best.

> *The problem with falling in love with someone who's just like you is that later on, all of a sudden, it hits you, and you realize what the problem is: You can't be with someone like yourself.*
>
> *You hate yourself!*

Infact, if anything you need is to get the exact opposite of your-self. It's too much. It's too much!

Perhaps being with people just like me would make me a little cra-zy too. How about you?

Mind, Body, Spirit

When I went for my master's degree in counseling, I was following the holistic track. What this meant was we needed to look at people and their issues and concerns across the contexts of their mind, body, and spirit. In my own heart I believe this to be true and of utmost importance, and yet we so often forget to discuss it explicitly. This was my chance to say something about it.

Posted: 11/17/2015

There could have been more damage on this journey. Much more!

There were many crossroads along the path; there were many winding turns that often returned me to the place where I started

Sometimes, the car went off the road; the train jumped the tracks, and sometimes I was just out of gas. The bumps, the bruises not only impacted me, but also the many people who shared different parts of the journey. Some stayed and some left. For each of those who shared my journey, some of the bumps and bruises healed and some have left scars of various depths. Perhaps this is true for everyone's life, but for most of the time, I could not focus past myself.

Looking back, I don't think it could have been any different, and after a deep breath and a big sigh, I can admit that it was just perfect the way it was.

— ☼ —

A few years ago, when I first started speaking about my experience, I was asked to talk about my journey from the perspective of integrating my mind, body, and spirit for a group of graduate counseling students.

I started to think about all the different issues that were the constant chatter inside of me and which dimension of my spirit, my mind, and my body was the source. It looked like this...

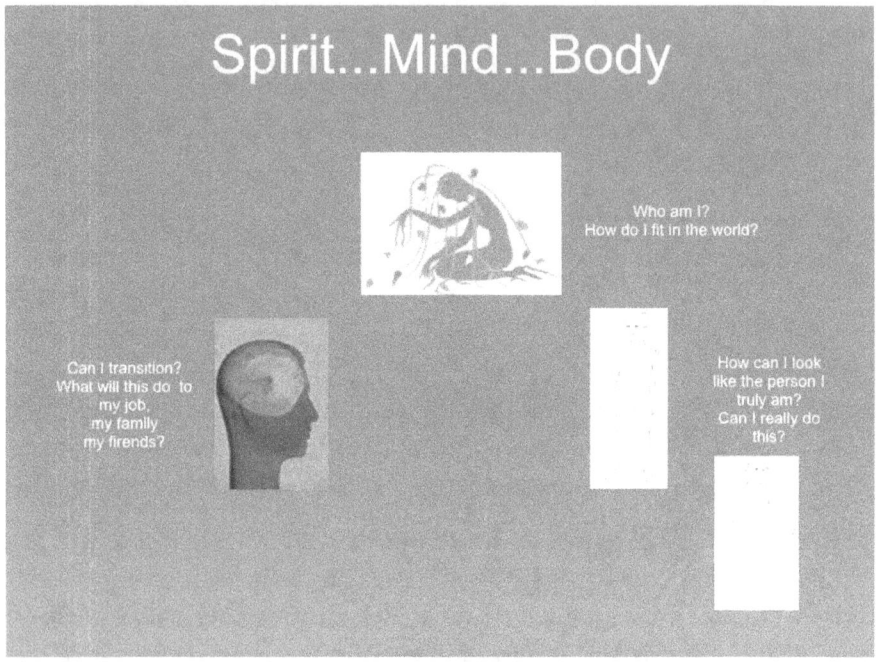

Mind, spirit, body chatter.

As long as I can remember, my spirit was never at rest. Before I went to kindergarten I had no sense that boys and girls were separated. I was just a child, and even now cannot remember a real sense of my gender identity. But once school started, and the boys and girls were often separated, especially when they went to play, something did not feel right. It was a feeling, and I was confused, even way back then, without having a clue what this was all about. Over time, there was chatter in my head, a very low level, perhaps just a whisper that was questioning: Who am I? Where do I fit?

Then I learned how to play with the other boys—and even then, it was not an easy journey. The battle between my gender identity and my sexual orientation was a spiritual dilemma for so much of my life. My spirit felt that it was at war with my body, and there was never a solution that seemed possible. At least it felt that way for so long.

My body lied to me all my life. Way back in 1960 at my Bar Mitzvah, part of me was looking forward to getting my first electric razor to remove those wispy hairs that were showing that "today, I am a man," was battling with the spirit inside of me that was yelling how wrong this all was, as I still heard those whispers. But mixed in, I could also hear some crying. But I was getting tough—perhaps even a bully of sorts—and knew I had to let the boy become the man and be strong in order to survive. I knew it was the only option.

My mind knew there was only one way. I got married, became a father, raised the kids, provided as well and as best I could while keeping the voices and the chatter in the background as suppressed as I could. When I was alone, I could dream and felt obsessed and compelled to let my spirit have some freedom, and found some pieces of women's clothing. Sometimes this was sufficient to put the "fire" out for the moment; sometimes it didn't.

For decade upon decade, my spirit, mind, and body were at war with each other. I lived in many worlds—my career, my family—all while hiding so much of myself for fear of people learning this about me. I was an actor who wore so many masks to face the world and was probably not the best person I could be to anyone.

I was working hard to be the person I thought they needed me to be. Even when they wanted more than I was giving, I denied it and would fight, reject, and project on them that they were wrong. Certainly I was hiding all of this to myself and never had a sense that I might be causing wounds to those I cared about.

I was married for 25 years and raised three children. Even after my divorce, the war between my mind, body, and spirit continued for another decade before I could face the problem and find the solution of alignment. My denial had to end, and the possibilities to accept that I was trans, and that I could and would do something to align my body to my spirit, and then was surprised as to how the chatter, the whispers, the crying in the crevices of my mind stopped as all was aligned.

I consider myself blessed to reach this alignment. It would be easy to dwell in regret, but I am pretty sure the alignment of all of me finds no reason to go there.

I am at peace now, and can look back at the journey that got me here and know it was perfect.

I am at peace now and look forward to the next journey.

Making Every Day Thanksgiving

I try to be timely and it was Thanksgiving time. I already mentioned how much gratitude I have in my life. I cannot talk about this too often!

Posted: 11/23/2015

It is hard to be thankful when you are not living your truth.

It has taken me a long time to figure this out…and then some more time to do something about it.

Being grateful; living in gratitude; being thankful; living in thanksgiving, are not concepts that come naturally. It seems to me even when taught to us, many struggle with allowing these core values to become part of our being, rather than lofty goals that only others may achieve as we focus on our own personal stories and challenges. Perhaps we may admire those who can live in gratitude, but for some reason we may not be fully inspired enough so that we will also. At least that was part of my journey.

It has taken some time to pay attention to those teachers out in the world who have inspired me. I was so resistant for such a long time. I made believe that I had my life together, and fooled a lot of people. Most of all, I now understand how much I was fooling myself.

I used to hear the words, made famous by Joseph Campbell, "Follow your Bliss." It took me a while to really understand what he meant. In an excerpt from *Moyers Moments,* from "Joseph Campbell and The Power of Myth, Episode 4: Sacrafice and Bliss," you can listen here: (https://www.youtube.com/watch?v=QHBBplGmLbM)

Bliss 01 2

On *Moyer's Moments*, Joseph Campbell, "Follow Your Bliss"

I always tell my students to follow your bliss. Follow your bliss. Where the deep sense of being in form and where your body and soul want to go. When you have that feeling, then stay with it and don't let anyone throw you off.

I found another clip of him when he was pressed to define bliss once again, and he clearly stated that your bliss is your authenticity. Once I heard that, it totally made sense, and this student was ready. Yes, I was scared, but I began to understand it was the only answer for me.

— ☼ —

Back in 2002 to 2003, I did a lot of personal growth work. I was newly single once again. I was struggling with my identity and identities, and still not at peace with my dysphoria, and searching for some answers and direction. One of the teachers/facilitators I met kept repeating a message that also took me some time to let it sink in. She advised all the participants that: "The pit stop in hell is optional."

Wow! We have a choice in this. We can live in the past or live with the old stories and beliefs—or not! It also took me time to get this message and start to live with it too. I think I am almost there—not sure if I will ever get fully there—but I do now know it is my choice, and being a victim of the universe is not something I choose to be.

I realize that throughout my life there have been many teachers available to me. Some did not even know they were teaching me something, and from many, I did not even know I was being taught. Every now and again, a memory lights up a corner of my brain, and I catch a glimpse of some lesson that has been stored away for me to find—to remember—and with fresh eyes, I see it with both astonishment and now a willingness to acknowledge the lesson it is and has been, as it patiently waited for me to come along for it.

This is how I have finally learned about gratitude and thanksgiving as more than just words but as a feeling that touches all of my mind, body, and spirit. I am glad that I have now reached that point in my life. I have no regrets that it took so long. After all, isn't dwelling in regret just spending time in that pit stop I mentioned earlier?

I am so grateful to have this life I am having—each and every minute of it. To me, every day is one of thanksgiving.

For many people, reaching the age of 64 means a time to relax, a time to retire. For me it was the time to start living as my true self. That was four short years ago, and my life is so very different now. I know I am one of the very lucky one's who has lost no one as I took this journey to live my truth. There is not a single day that I do not appreciate this. I am in gratitude and full of thanksgiving each day. I regret nothing and look forward to all the lessons that still may be trapped inside of me, and the new ones being offered everywhere I turn. I am so grateful to have this life I am having—each and every minute of it. To me, every day is one of thanksgiving.

"Grateful," by Nimo Patel, Daniel Nahmod

A few years ago I found this video, and I would like to share it with you for this week of Thanksgiving. It is called *Grateful: Love Song to the World* (https://www.youtube.com/watch?v=sO2o98Zpzg8).

I'll leave you here, and wish each of you a Happy Thanksgiving, and perhaps you may be still signing the chorus...

All that I am
All that I see
All that I've been
And all that I'll ever be...

Downloading a Friend

A wonderful, unexpected and unique life experience occurred. I thought it was worthy of sharing. I hope you agree.

Posted 12/02/2015

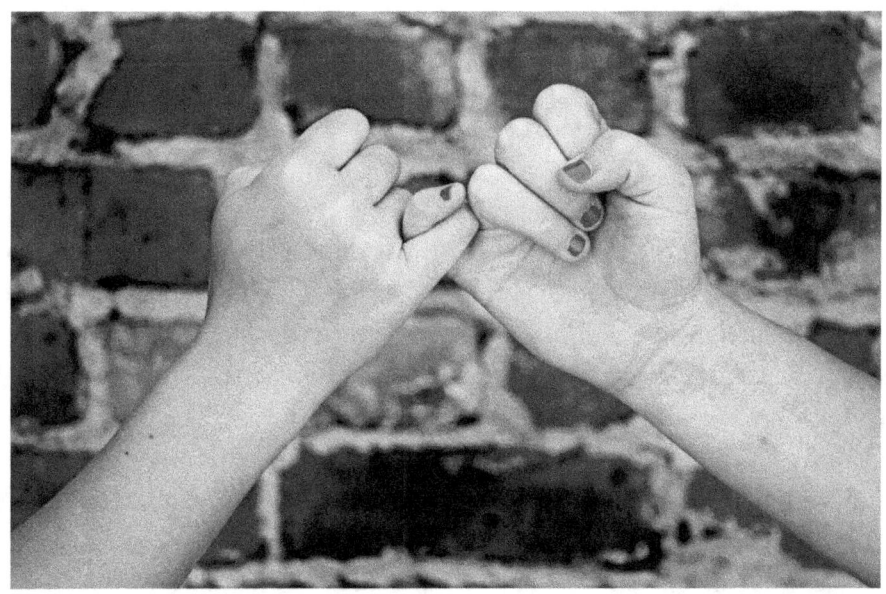

Friends.

Before I came to terms and self-acceptance with my truth, I spent over 40 years working as a design engineer and engineering manager. I used to think as each Friday rolled around, and usually by noontime, most people would start to relax and unwind and get ready for the weekend. I quickly learned that this was not necessarily the way things were in that world I was in. Friday's became a day of wariness, dread, and I always found myself on high alert, before the all clear signal rang and I was able to even consider the weekend was a possibility.

Some of you may know what I am referring to; what I call the "Friday at 3:00 p.m. problem." When this happened, all bets, all plans were off. Disappointment took over for my family and me and almost never could be explained or repaired. This more often happened when I worked in various startup companies, but also was part of the culture in larger established companies. The company, the project, the schedule, the customer, always came first. Yet, this was the life, the career that I chose. It never mattered if this happened on a regular basis or not; the possibility of it was always in the air, and the threat of disappointment was always heavy each Friday.

– ☼ –

I have been out of the tech world for a little over two years as I am writing this, but last week, I had one of those problems that occurred just before a long weekend was approaching. Last Wednesday around 3:00 p.m. This was the afternoon before Thanksgiving so it certainly fits the "Friday at 3:00 p.m. problem" definition. I found that a very important financial accounting file I needed was corrupted. Yes, I was triggered, and what made matters worse, I knew that I had been lax in keeping a backup file. (Please do not lecture me as to whether I have learned anything after 40 years in engineering. I feel crappy enough about this.)

The good part about being somewhat removed from my previous life, is that I was able to ignore the problem during Thursday and Friday of the holiday, but I knew there was a phone call that I was dreading to make. Yes, I was dreading it for so many reasons.

– ☼ –

So many reasons!

o I was using an application that was old and no longer supported. I would need to purchase an upgrade and had been avoiding this for some time

o It was pretty embarrassing to admit I had no backup file.

o It was an application used by The Tiffany Club of New England (TCNE), and registered to another person, long gone from the club, and I was not even certain what name it was registered under, so I knew I would need to explain about TCNE being a transgender support group

o Calling any customer service line is always an adventure and a test of my voice with the risk of being mis-gendered over the phone, and then to see where that adventure may lead. So far my record seems to be 50-50 on how I am responded to by gender, even with stating my name as Grace…. This in itself is an interesting phenomenon.

On Saturday morning, I went to the Microsoft store in a local mall where I have built a relationship with some of the peeps there, and although he cleaned up my PC a little, he could not access the corrupted file and told me what I already knew—and dreaded—I would need to call the customer support number. I struggled a little longer; trying to put it off some more, while looking at the website where it said available 24/7. It was around 3:00 p.m. on Saturday afternoon that I took a deep breath, started to dial the number.

Each of my concerns above was realized during the call, but one by one, I/we got through them and then something totally unexpected happened, something that was so miraculous, it totally restored my faith in humanity. I just have to share it with you.

I was connected to a support person. She had a pleasant voice but it was pretty clear we were going through the standard script. I provided my name, but was still getting a response of "sir." I let this go a few times as I thought it was not the main purpose of the call (you might think differently on this). I was able to find the license number of the application software. I did have to explain TCNE as a transgender support group and go through possible male and female names for the original buyer. Luckily I found the person's old email address that provided the required confirmation. Then the adventure really began.

I corrected the technician the next time I was "sir'ed" and received genuine apology. I asked if she was familiar with transgender people and she clearly was, and sounded knowledgeable and supportive, so that provided a great sense of relief that I would get through this. As expected, I needed to purchase an upgrade package, and asked if she could just download it for me. She took control of my PC and it appeared that the download would take over an hour to complete. As she watched and controlled my PC she started to ask me what kind of work that TCNE did as a support group. This was totally unexpected and so much better than music on hold for an hour. She told me how difficult it was for people in her area that were "different." I asked her where she was. I was shocked to learn that she was in the Philippines, and it was almost four in the morning for her. We chatted for a while and shared and learned so much about each other while this software was downloading. I shared my website and pointed her to some of my blogs. We learned we are so very different, yet we both have a similar center of love and acceptance even when those around us may not have these same beliefs. We connected in a number of ways during this download.

I have made a new friend, halfway across the world.

Not only did I download a new application, I downloaded a new friend.

Perhaps those Friday at 3:00 p.m. problems are not so bad after all!

Superstar

As I am writing this introduction the December 8, 2015 post in March 2016, there have been a number of people of my generation who have left us. Holly Woodlawn, although not a famous entertainment figure, was a so-called Warhol Superstar back from those days when I had parts so lost, confused, and hidden. This is another article that was spontaneous when I heard of her death. I am not sure many understood, but it felt right for me to write about it.

Posted: 12/08/2015

Holly Woodlawn.
Photo credit: Angela George.

There were so many phrases and titles flitting and flying through my consciousness this past week. I love and sit in joy and amazement watching how one of these ideas will jump out above the others and flesh into one of these little stories that I share with you. Sometimes, they take over and start writing themselves, and sometimes I force myself to open the file and just watch my fingers as they start to dance over the keyboard.

This past weekend, I had a few ideas that were sitting on Post-it Notes, my white board, or just floating around my mind—yet I had no clarity which one would cry for its freedom to become whole.

I woke up this Monday morning, December 7, which has its own infamous place in history and felt disconnected from my blog. I was empty and decided to put writing on hold today, and just do some cleaning and plant repotting.

Then.... I first saw it on Facebook, and then here on Huffington Post. Holly Woodlawn has passed.

Yesterday, I was happily nostalgic as I heard a DJ say it was the fiftieth anniversary of the Beatles album *Rubber Soul*. Probably millions or even billions of people will know that reference. On Facebook I exchanged so many memories of records and songs that the day finished on a pleasant note.

Today, I am trying to assess my feelings to Holly's passing and wondering how many people even know that she was a real person.

I never was brave enough to take that "Walk on the Wild Side," but living in confusion and hiding in my teens and twenties—and for the next four decades also, it was important to see Holly and the Warhol culture of Superstars, even if I had no idea how or if it related to my very own life.

They were different, they were queer (oh my god—I said it!), they were in your face, they were troubled, but most important, they were public. I was confused and afraid. I am not sure whether they made me more or less confused and afraid, but I knew I was glad they were there.

I graduated from college in 1969, and moved to Boston for my first job as an engineer. I remember persuading many of my newfound friends to go in the seedy neighborhood of Boston to see Warhol's *Trash*. There is nothing like taking new friends to see something like this. I will never forget it. All while I was getting very good at hiding in plain sight.

— ☼ —

plucked her eyebrows on the way,
shaved her legs, then he was a she...

– Lou Reed, "Walk on the Wild Side"

Oh how I dreamed it could be so simple! But the Warhol Superstars were not real people, right. They were not like you and me, with real lives, real bills, real friends, real family, and real commitments. They drank, they drugged, and they sold themselves. Or—was that a story that I used to protect myself? Even if it was true. Superstars shine brightly but they burn out too.

$$- \diamond -$$

I am still trying to understand how I feel about this news. I wonder if Holly Woodlawn was a happy person. Did she really live her truth? I have an image planted in my brain of her from the movie *Trash* that is not pleasant. Was that a movie or an early reality show? I am not sure, I really want to know.

What I do know is that by allowing herself to be seen, way back 45 to 50 years ago, this made a difference to me. Mostly by letting me know that even though I did not understand that internal conflict within me, there were others with similar if not identical conflict. I have talked much about how we are all unique like snowflakes. Even Superstars are unique snowflakes.

Holly Woodlawn's Super Star will always shine bright to me. RIP.

Dys-informed

I like playing with words. I like combining them and even trying to make them up. It seems to me every trans person may think of themselves as an expert on the topic of gender variance. The media is both good and bad trying to explain what gender variance is all about. Here, I tried to raise the conversation ever so slightly, and through a different lens. Again, I am never sure if I am successful in these endeavors.

Posted: 12/15/2015

A few years ago, when I was in graduate school for my counseling psychology master's degree, right in the middle of a psychopathology class, I had a classmate who proudly announced that she was "OC without the D." She happily claimed that she was obsessive and compulsive, yet considered it a good thing, and not a disorder. For me that was a quiet learning moment that I could relate too, in ways I was not yet ready to announce to my classmates.

A few years later I was happy to get a diagnosis that was labeled a disorder, but I knew that there was really nothing wrong with me. After all, my very experienced gender therapist stated very clearly that what I needed to do was the only way to live my life with "full effectiveness." Hindsight certainly proves her assessment correct.

A few years later, with the publication of the *Diagnostic and Statistical Manual of Mental Disorders, Fifth Edition* (DSM-5), the diagnosis name was changed to gender dysphoria. Some people were happy to take the word "disorder" out of the diagnosis, while others argued it was still laden with many issues.

After completing a lengthy assessment and after years of experience diagnosing patients with gender conditions, it is my professional opinion that Ms. Stevens is diagnosed with DSM IV Gender Identity Disorder codified as 302.85 and is a transsexual. As such, I believe the only effective treatment for her is a combination of psychotherapy, medical, and surgical intervention by enable her to live as a female—the only role in which she can function comfortably and with full effectiveness.

From letter supporting my gender reassignment surgery.

For me, I was ecstatic, at the time of my diagnosis as for many like me, that diagnosis, that letter, was the key we needed to move to the place in our lives we knew we had to. Personally I did not care much about the label, as I had my classmate's definition firmly planted in my brain—I could have "issues" with my gender identity, but it was not a disorder. This worked for me but I understood it did not necessarily work for everyone else.

– ☼ –

Now, fast forwarding to the past few years where we have gender variance and transgender talked about daily in the various forms of media, the plethora of both reality and dramatic TV shows featuring transgender people, I suspect the general public may be getting an overload of information on this part of the population that I am part of. There are so many stories, so many possibilities, so many ways that we are gender variant, that even being in the trans community, I still marvel at the uniqueness of each person's journey, opinions, and view. It would be so nice if there were a neat box that we could wrap up and put under our holiday tree to inform everyone what it is like to be transgender.

We are told to tell and share our stories, and tell them we must and we should. There are as many stories as there are people, and some day, I dream, that the world will understand that the story of each of our own unique versions of gender dysphoria is not so much different than each person's personal story of their own life. Our stories do not fit into a small box. Our stories are ongoing, living realities, which move, change, and hopefully grow. I like to think of our stories the same way we think of investing in the stock market, where we are warned that past performance does not predict future performance. We do not need to be trapped in our story, we can write a new chapter each and every moment. In fact, I think we must, as this is what being alive really means! Oh, and this is not for just for those of us who may be transgender—it is for everyone.

– ☼ –

That psychopathology class I took, in one sense was teaching us to get a better understanding of the boxes and labels the "greater minds" collected in *Diagnostic and Statistical Manual of Mental Disorders, Fourth Edition* (DSM-IV) that was used at that time. The most important learning I received in that class was not these boxes and labels, but when the professor stated that for our clients, their diagnosis would depend on which side of the Charles River (either the Cambridge or the Boston side) the counselor was. Observing the sides, the politics and negotiation to create DSM 5, brings me back to that main learning I received about the labels of diagnosis, which to me, lessened the value of the label.

So I have a diagnosis of gender identity disorder (GID). I needed it to move forward. Was I gender dysphoric? I think that is a strong affirmative. Was my experience the same as others? Probably this is somewhat true and somewhat not true. Could I explain this in a way others could easily understand? Probably not! I am pretty sure this may be true for everyone.

Whether or not you are transgender, I suggest there is really no way to hear only one story, or even hundreds or thousands of stories and come away with one single map that gives you the picture of what it is like to be gender variant, or not fit the gender binary model or transgender. Sure it would be simpler, but the fact is that it is far from simple, and that is OK!

If you keep insisting there is only one way for you to understand, I suggest you just may be...dys-informed.

Trans-expectations

Another hyphenated title had me excited. I am not sure why. This is another view about personal evolution and change, one of my favorite themes.

Posted: 12/21/2015

> *It's a little bit funny this feeling inside*
> *I'm not one of those who can easily hide*

– Elton John, "Your Song"

I spent decades trying to understand those feelings inside of me. Whenever I came close to finding the words to describe them, to own them, I would push them back into hiding, as I was so scared of what it would mean. No matter how hard I pushed them down, they always pushed their way back up to the surface of my being, seeking to be free and open in their truth. They would not easily hide—no not easily at all!

In my early sixties, I finally was able to say the word "transsexual" and claim it as one of my many identities. However, I also knew that there were still so many feelings inside that I could not find the right words to articulate. I knew I was female. It was my sense of being, perhaps my soul. I know I am female! I still am not quite certain how to put this in words. It has taken me the past few years to accept that I may never have the words to explain, to describe, to articulate this feeling inside and realize that it does not in any way diminish my sense of self.

However, when I transitioned, it was different. I had a few expectations—actually it would be better to describe them as dreams and
wishes. I knew it would be challenging for my (adult) kids, and my co-
workers. I knew that I would need to discover myself—my style, my
clothes, my makeup and had no idea what it would be like waking up
each day and just getting dressed rather than "dressing up." The fact is
that this all took some time to figure out. For me, returning to work
gave me the classic—and somewhat surreal 15 minutes of fame, as I
was the topic du jour before things settled down. I was fascinated to
watch people's reactions over time, and see which of my co-workers
would come closer, drift off into the distance, or keep the relationship
pretty much the same.

Like many of us who transition, I had hoped that nothing much
would change. However, my journey did not quite work out that way.
Even the relationships that appeared not to change, in many ways did,
and what was most surprising, was recognizing the slow changes in
myself. I was learning how to "be" for a second time. It took me a
while to learn that this work was mine, and mine alone. I did not expect this back then, but I did learn so much from it. Perhaps changing
gender was the easy part of my transition—learning how to be the real
me, has proved to be the ongoing journey of my life.

A friend who recently transitioned has been sharing some of her
journey and appears to be going through the common stage of asking
herself—and all her friends—what defines one as a woman. I remember when I went through that part of my journey and found it challenging to move from being externally validated to become internally
validated and to learn to fully accept that I am happy being me and
comfortable in my own skin.

I know I am not the first person to recognize that each person's
journey is unique, and how hard it is to describe our feelings inside. It
has been so hard for me to recognize that I may never have the words

to describe my own internal feelings, yet I have talked with so many people who find themselves in desperate need for the words to help them navigate their journey. I consider myself lucky that I was able to let go of that need but recognize that others may not be able to.

− ☼ −

I am pretty sure that each of us, whether trans or not, have our dreams, our expectations of what our lives will be like. For some, the dreams come true, for others the journey may take a different path.

Your path is yours alone, and I would never tell you what you "should" do, However, I can share what I have learned on my journey as someone who has made a major life change late in life and is now embracing change, adventure, and learning to let go of expectations:

I do not subscribe to regrets and looking back to what I either had or did not have, who I was or who I was not.

I subscribe that we have only this moment in time, to make choices to be the best person (note—no gender marker here) we can be. I am female (totally internally validated) and that sense of myself is sufficient for me.

I do not have to be a certain way to meet any cultural expectations. I do recognize that the internal war that went on for so long was necessary to make me who I am NOW.

My history and my experiences, if I am lucky, may have helped me gain wisdom, but most of all has enabled me to now be willing to learn something new.

All women ask the same questions. This is not an issue just for trans women. I recently went to a weekend retreat with 40-plus women seeking to find their own version of what it means to be a woman.

You can define your own version of what it is to be the woman that you uniquely are. From a feminist perspective, you can choose to be any version of woman that you want.

Enjoy your journey.

Not Then, Not When, the Magic of Now!

What better way to end my first calendar year of weekly writing than to quote "The Circle Game?" I always loved this picture that my son took a few years ago and thought it would be perfect. Since I have already established that I time travel, trying to stay present is also something I have to work at, and share with all of you.

Posted: 12/31/2015

And the seasons they go round and round
And the painted ponies go up and down
We're captive on the carousel of time....

– Joni Mitchell, "The Circle Game"

The carousel goes round and round... Photo credit: Simi Rabinowitz.

The old year 2015 is ending and the New Year 2016 will soon begin. Like the Roman god Janus, we spend some time looking back at what has occurred in our lives—the good; the bad; the opportunities not taken; and the blessings we received. Like the Roman god Janus we spend some time looking ahead at our dreams and wishes, and if inspired enough, we may even set some goals for the future.

I know what it is like to have dreams and wishes without setting any goals, or planning to take any action. It has taken a long time to just learn from the past rather than to continue to live in it. It has taken me a long time to live in the present and not get lost in my dreams of possible futures. I have learned that the universe truly does reward action, and the action must be taken by us.

We can believe in magic, but we must be the magicians of our own lives! We must be the one to cast the spell, and wave our wands. We may be like the students at Hogwarts, where, as we are learning to do this, the outcomes are not quite what we wanted, but over time and repetition, I dare say we learn to become more effective in our actions.

We learn to initiate our spells, and we learn to adapt to the outcomes as they occur. This is the true wizardry and wisdom of life. No one can do it for us, and we each will learn it when we are ready.

There is truly magic in the present moment...the moment of *now*! This moment seems to fly by so quickly yet is always there! Once we can learn that the times of *then* and *when* are nice places to occasionally visit, we can enjoy this magic in each and every *now*. This trick is not easily learned, and even when it is learned is often forgotten. I often get trapped in the *then* and *when* and have to work hard to find my way back to *now*.

However, I have learned that every trip I make to my past or one of my possible futures has a lesson in it. Sometimes it takes me many trips to recognize the lesson and what I can do in the *now* once I learn it. Sometimes the lesson provides a clear call to action, and sometimes the lesson is a bit gentler and gives me a view of appreciation that I had lacked before. I would like to share one of these trips to *then*.

Looking back: 1959. It was the summer I was turning 12. Perhaps you might remember what an awkward age that is—somewhere between being a child and a teenager. Puberty was beginning and I was clueless and confused as to all the inner feelings and battles going on. It was the last summer my parents sent me off to day camp. I fought so hard with my parents that I no longer wanted to go to the camp I had gone to the previous four years. They got it and we found a new camp that was in one of the Coney Island baths. This was heaven! Each day after lunch the entire group got to go out on the boardwalk and spend time in the various arcades and rides. I loved playing skeeball, which I argued was a game of skill, and also rolling the balls on the electromechanical poker games. At 12 years old this felt so grown up.

However, each trip ended at the carousel. Yes, the carousel had those painted ponies that went up and down, but it was much more than that. This was not a passive treat, but it was an active competition among all my friends in the group. Each time around there was a mechanical arm that held rings that could be grabbed if your pony was in the proper position and you were coordinated enough to lean over and grab and pull the ring out of the mechanism that held it. Most of the rings were a silver colored metal. If you were lucky and skilled you just might have the chance to catch a golden ring. Getting the gold ring entitled you to another free ride on the carousel and if you caught it, that it was better than getting any number of silver rings.

– ☼ –

I know that my life has been so blessed and I have been so lucky. My painted ponies have and still do go up and down....up and down.... Yes, just like you, I am captive on the carousel of time.....but I have been lucky enough to catch a gold ring, and have been blessed to receive this free ride to live my truth, and learn the magic of *now*.

I hope that each of you capture your own gold ring. There are plenty for all!

Have a happy and wonderful New Year.

– ☼ –

A giant and heartfelt thank you to all of you who have been reading and shar-ing my writings in 2015. Each week has been magical to me. Be True!

Afterword

I have been writing the entire year under the "brand" of My Transgender Life. Perhaps I could have just called it "My Life," but then I suspect it would lose some of its attraction to people.

I dream that more than just those in the transgender community would read these weekly short stores and find something in their life they could relate to. Perhaps something I said at one time or another, would plant a seed of inspiration to move forward on living authentically. Perhaps it would just begin with a "musing" rather than an immediate call to action. That's even more than OK with me.

It took me sometime to realize that most of what I write has a structure to it. I never planned it and am fascinated to see how it creates itself.

I usually start with an invitation to some topic, and follow with a personal story of my own life and experience. More often than not I may offer a moral or lesson to what I may have learned from my experiences. I try hard to finish with another invitation, but this one is more of a call to action to look into your own life and investigate your own position and what lesson you have learned and need to move forward on. My hope is that this is true whether you are in the trans community or not. Many people have told me that this is true for them so I hope I am on the right track.

It is not easy to let go of our secrets or follow our dreams. I know how our fears of disconnection get in the way.

For those of us that have made the decision, the choice to live our truth, our authentic lives, perhaps it is best to repeat the term that LaVerne Cox shared. We are possibility models.

The take away is:

Nothing is impossible!

Acknowledgments

I find it so interesting to have a part of me who acts as an observer to watch my own evolution, and I have learned to build a relationship with him. Sometimes he is quite direct with his observations, while there are also times that he just smiles at me with little to say. This used to trigger a few parts that were getting angry, until I learned that his real goal was to help bring forward as many parts as would be open to be inspired by any and all sources. It was only then, that I was able to return smile for smile.

For the past three years, I have been attending the monthly local New England chapter meetings of the National Speakers Association. I learned to attend with a beginner's mind, and although expecting nothing, was amazed by the gems I learned from each of the guest speakers, and the openness of all the attendees. I would be remiss if I did not acknowledge the synergism of going to these meetings to aid my evolution as a speaker and writer of these random musings. Perhaps it is a bit nonspecific, but this group is a village that has taught me a great deal.

There is also another village: all of my friends who come by The Tiffany Club of New England each week. There have been many stories that have provided inspiration for my writing, to share, to teach as I hope I have done within these pages. The feedback I receive is also invaluable to keep me going week after week.

A book such as this, bringing my earlier writings together, takes a special editor/book "person" and once again I deeply thank Claudia Gere for her support and creativeness and overall ability to question me, guide me, and let me know if some of my thoughts seem to make any sense to a broader audience, as I will so often get a bit lost in the layers I play with.

I have a deep thanks to Rabbi Michael Bernstein who was kind enough to provide the Foreword here. He has become a resource that I can bounce ideas off of, and I love to read his blogs and postings to help me evolve my spiritual center from being transparent, to translucent, to trans-visible, and to what I hope will become trans-luminent.

There have been people from all over the world who have contacted me in response to some of these musings, letting me know that I touched something in them and perhaps made a small difference in their life. I want to thank these people who reached out to me, as I do believe that is the real reason I keep writing.

– Grace Stevens

May 2016

Grace's Next Book, Coming Soon
THE ALPHABET OF SELF
GRACE ANNE STEVENS

For children ages 4 to 104, *The Alphabet of Self*, teaches both the vocabulary of feelings and how to articulate them without being overpowered by them.

Modeling and assimilating the language, children and adults together will learn experientially to be self-led.

Books Sure to Empower Women in the New Year

By Joan Schweighardt

No! Maybe? Yes! Living My Truth
By Grace Anne Stevens

Book reviewer Alice Bouvrie was the first of many to call *No! Maybe? Yes! Living My Truth* by Grace Anne Stevens "the best account of what it means to be a woman that [she] had ever read." That's quite a powerful statement, especially in Grace's case, because Grace was actually born with the physical attributes of a man.

This memoir takes readers deep inside Grace's head, where they are immediately privy to the same internal and conflicting voices that Grace had to listen to since childhood. Grace transitioned at age 64 and is currently 68. That means she was born in the dark ages, before the Internet, before Caitlyn Jenner and Jennifer Boylan, back in the days when telling people you were not who you appeared to be could get you institutionalized. But her book is more expansive than that, moving well beyond the boundaries of her own unique and thrilling journey. The lessons she learned along the way are applicable to every woman seeking authenticity, whether she is crossing the great gender divide or simply reexamining how far she may have strayed from her truest self. Grace Stevens, an author/speaker/trainer who writes a weekly blog for *Huff Post* (entitled "My Transgender Life"), is a passionate and engaging writer. If her well-written memoir doesn't inspire you to move closer to the kind of life you can celebrate daily, nothing will.

Grace invites you to purchase your copy of

No! Maybe? Yes! Living My Truth

Paperback, 262 pages, $19.95
Available on Amazon and other bookstores

To purchase in bulk at discount prices,
contact the author:

Email: gas333@verizon.net
phone: (781) 789-6103

Grace Anne Stevens
Inspiring People to Find Their Truth and Live Their Authentic Life!

Grace Stevens is an inspirational and motivational speaker specializing on intra and interpersonal relationships to improve individual and group performance in all aspects of people's lives.

Grace's skill of simplifying psychological concepts mixed with sharing personal stories provides a unique and lasting experience for her audience. Listen to Grace and what it means to Live Your Truth: http://www.graceannestevens.com/livingontrack.cfm

Invite Grace to Speak to Your Group
www.graceannestevens.com

About the Author

Grace Stevens is an inspirational and motivational speaker specializing in personal transformation as well as intra- and interpersonal relationships to improve all aspects of individual and group performance.

With her experience in corporate technical management, individual and group counseling, and as an author and speaker, Grace has made a difference in people's lives worldwide.

Grace started her career as an engineer designing computers for missile guidance systems. At the age of fifty-eight, while still working in the tech world, she returned to school and earned a Master's Degree in Counseling Psychology from Lesley University in 2009. She was dual careered as she continued working evenings in a substance abuse clinic until 2015.

Grace is a transgender woman who transitioned gender at the age of sixty-four successfully in two vastly different workplaces, the technical and counseling worlds. Grace strongly believes, "We are all so much more than just gender."

Grace is an active leader and board member of The Tiffany Club of New England, a 501(c)(3) charitable organization, which is one of the country's largest transgender support groups. She has been one of the co-leaders of their annual conference, First Event, since 2011. She has presented workshops and advised many people on their change journeys. Grace received a 2012 Community Involvement award from EMC Corporation for her work with The Tiffany Club of New England.

Grace is a regular contributor to *The Huffington Post* with her blogs on "My Transgender Life," where she continues to share her experiences and inspire people from all walks of life. She has also been interviewed on radio, TV, and newspapers.

Grace has written two books; *No! Maybe? Yes! Living My Truth,* and *Musings on Living Authentically.* She is presently writing a book to introduce the concepts of parts to children in *The Alphabet of Self.*

Grace's website is www.graceannestevens.com. Read more from Grace on: http://www.huffingtonpost.com/grace-anne-stevens/.

www.ingramcontent.com/pod-product-compliance
Lightning Source LLC
Chambersburg PA
CBHW070600130626
46556CB00001B/231